Tucson Cooks!

Tucson Cooks!

An Extraordinary Culinary Adventure

Tucson's finest independent restauranteurs share
their stories, menus, recipes and kitchens to benefit
The Primavera Foundation.

Special Thanks

The Primavera Foundation Cookbook Committee would like to thank the following individuals and organizations for their generous support and encouragement of the *Tucson Cooks!* project:

AC Productions, Godat Design, Pastiche Modern Eatery, Perfection Plastic Surgery P.C., The Schroeder Family, and the University of Arizona Press

Primavera Foundation Cookbook Committee

Meghan Brown, Cathalena Burch, Pat Connors, Art Clifton, Lynn Hassler, Holly Lachowicz, and Sue Myal

Library of Congress Catalog Card Number: 2005907494
ISBN 9780964361355

Printed in the USA
First Printing 2005

Design: Leticia Craig-Welch, Godat Design

The Primavera Foundation, Inc.
702 South 6th Avenue, Tucson, AZ 85701
520.623.5111

Table of Contents

8   Introduction

10   Restaurant Index

11   Recipe Index

17   Participating Restaurants, Stories, Menus and Recipes

115 Other Tucson Originals Restaurants

About Tucson Cooks!

For four years, Tucson has hosted a series of summer dining events know as Primavera Cooks! In Tucson Cooks! you will find stories, recipes and photographs about the collaboration between the Primavera Foundation and Tucson Originals that made these culinary events possible.

Tucson Cooks! highlights the Tucson Originals restaurants that hosted apprentice "hobby" chefs. These apprentices were willing to pay for the opportunity to work in gourmet restaurant kitchens with well known chefs. These chefs are responsible for some of the finest local cuisine. The chefs and apprentices planned, prepared and served a multi-course wine-paired dinner for approximately 50 guests. The dinners took place on different days at the different Tucson restaurants for four summers. Guests included friends of the apprentices, friends of the restaurants and Tucson Community members who wanted to support the efforts of these two well-respected, local, nonprofit organizations.

Inside Tucson Cooks! you'll find menus, recipes and wines for each event. You'll enjoy photographs of the chefs and apprentices working in the restaurant kitchens. The words of one of the apprentices sums up the experience. "I never had so much fun working so hard for such a good cause". Also included in Tucson Cooks! are short descriptions of the Tucson Originals restaurants, with addresses, hours and more recipes. We hope Tucson Cooks! helps you experience some of the fun.

Tucson Originals, formed in 1998, has more than 30 restaurants. This alliance of locally-owned, independent restaurants contributes to the local economy and strives to preserve the unique flavors of Tucson. Tucson Originals is well respected for its philanthropic efforts. The Primavera Foundation was founded in 1982. It addresses the systematic causes of homelessness and near homelessness with job training, employment, housing, home ownership and advocacy. The proceeds from the events and the sale of this book benefit the Primavera Foundation. These two grassroots, non-profit organizations represent some of the finest parts of the Tucson Community.

Join us for this culinary expedition through sharp knives, hot stoves, and gourmet recipes!

Holly Lachowicz, Primavera Foundation
Pat Connors, Tucson Originals

The chefs have shared their recipes with you. We hope you enjoy them. If there are any inaccuracies, they are unintentional. Time may change the accuracy of some of the restaurant information so we suggest you call before your first visit.

Restaurants

116	Acacia at St. Philips
118	Barrio Food & Drink
18	Bistro Zin
120	Chad's Steakhouse & Saloon
26	CuVée World Bistro
122	Dakota Café & Catering
124	Eclectic Café
126	El Charro Café
34	Elle, a wine country restaurant
42	Feast Restaurant
52	Fuego Restaurant Bar & Grill
60	Ghini's French Caffe
64	The Grill at Hacienda del Sol
128	Intermezzo
72	Janos
130	J BAR
78	Jonathan's Tucson Cork
88	Kingfisher Bar & Grill
132	Livorno Country Bistro
134	Magpies Gourmet Pizza
136	Mama Louisa's Italian Restaurant
138	Miguel's
140	Papagayo Mexican Restaurant
98	Pastiche Modern Eatery
142	Ric's Cafe
144	Roma Caffé
108	Terra Cotta
146	Westward Look Resort Gold Room
148	Wildflower, New American Cuisine

Appetizers

113 Asian Shrimp Skewers — Terra Cotta
107 Bacon Wrapped Escargot — Pastiche
25 Chicken Satay — Bistro Zin
97 Creole Barbeque Shrimp — Kingfisher
91 House Smoked Ruby Trout — Kingfisher
45 Lobster, Corn and Scallion Bread Pudding — Feast
63 Pâté de campagne — Ghini's
105 Roasted Duck with Fresh Blackberries over Arugula Greens with a Walnut Oil Vinaigrette — Pastiche
25 Seared Tuna Canapé — Bistro Zin
37 Steamed Mussels with White Wine, Garlic and Herbs — Elle
101 Sun-dried Tomato Cream Cheese Spread — Pastiche
67 Tellicherri Pepper Crusted Breast of Duck Canapes — Hacienda del Sol
145 Tomato Basil Bruschetta — Roma Caffé
101 Tuna Olive Tapénade — Pastiche

Salads

129 Bistro Fillet Salad with Strawberry-Balsamic Dressing — Intermezzo
31 Blackberry Zinfandel Dressing — CuVée
111 Cactus Paddle Salad — Terra Cotta
121 Chad's Famous Blue Cheese Salad Dressing — Chad's
143 Citrus Chipotle Vinaigrette — Ric's Cafe
29 Gorgonzola Gnocchi Salad — CuVée
47 Grapefruit Poppy Seed Dressing — Feast
85 Rock Shrimp, Cucumber and Raspberry Vinaigrette Salad — Jonathan's
37 Spinach Salad with Apple, Blue Cheese, Walnuts and Sherry Vinaigrette — Elle
125 Tahini Eggplant Salad with Mesquite Bacon — Eclectic Café

Soups and Sauces

59   Apricot Poblano Compote — Fuego
33   Cabernet Jus — CuVée
55   Cabernet Wine Jelly — Fuego
111 Corn and Poblano Soup — Terra Cotta
101 Don's Famous Gazpacho — Pastiche
143 Jack's Famous Green Chili Chicken Soup — Ric's Cafe
91   Melon Soup — Kingfisher
87   Remoulade Sauce — Jonathan's
127 Salsa de Chile Colorado — Red Enchilada Sauce — El Charro
83   Seasoned Salt — Jonathan's
119 Shrimp, Crab, Bacon, Saffron Jerk Bisque — Barrio
127 Sopa de Tortilla — El Charro
105 Vichyssoise With Chive Oil — Pastiche

Side Dishes

147 Asian Slaw — Westward Look
149 Asparagus Risotto — Wildflower
121 Chad's Cowboy Beans — Chad's
123 Corn Bake Casserole — Dakota Café
75   Creamy Polenta with Mascarpone — Janos
77   Glazed Minted Carrots — Janos
141 Green Corn Tamale Casserole — Papagayo's
77   Horseradish Mashed Potatoes — Janos
149 Macaroni and Cheese — Wildflower
23   Petite Beet Salad — Bistro Zin
55   Polenta Rounds — Fuego
107 Saffron Whipped Yukon Gold Potatoes — Pastiche
21   Salsify Granitée — Bistro Zin
71   Truffle Risotto — Hacienda del Sol

Main Dishes

117	Apricot, Honey Mustard Glazed Pork Loin – Acacia
133	Bleu Cheese Fillet – Livorno
51	Braised Pork with Clams and Vegetables – Feast
63	Capered Sole with Olives in Parchment – Ghini's
31	Carpaccio of Venison – CuVée
93	Cascabel Chile, Gulf Oyster and Fresh Chanterelle Pan Roast – Kingfisher
147	Charred Ahi Tuna – Westward Look
125	Chicken and Chorizo on Penne Pasta – Eclectic Café
133	Chicken Livorno – Livorno
135	Chicken Picante – Magpies
131	Chihuacle Chile and Citrus-based Salmon with Roasted Tomatillo Salsa – J BAR
117	Chipotle and Molasses Glazed Rotisserie Chicken – Acacia
23	Crispy Duck Breast with Fig Jus Poulet – Bistro Zin
59	Duck Confit – Fuego
83	Duck Galantine – Jonathan's
103	Grilled Lamb Chops with Garlic Balsamic Glaze – Pastiche
39	Grilled Lamb Chops with Herbed Risotto and Red Wine Butter Sauce – Elle
81	Lime Broiled Cabrilla with Roasted Red Chili Sauce – Jonathan's
119	Mango Pasta – Barrio
113	Maurice's Southwestern Duck à la Orange – Terra Cotta
41	Orecchiette Pasta with Chicken, Garlic Sausage, Mushrooms and Eggplant – Elle
55	Ostrich Sauté Cabernet – Fuego
145	Penne all'Arrabiata – Roma Caffé
105	Roasted Duck with Blackberries – Pastiche
139	Seafood Relleno – Miguel's
69	Seared Angus Fillet Mignon with Caramelized Shallot Jus – Hacienda del Sol
71	Seared Diver Scallops with Oven Roasted Pineapple and Mango Salsa – Hacienda del Sol

Main Dishes *Continued*

39	Seared Salmon with Roasted Vegetable Lasagna — Elle
49	Stuffed Softshell Crabs — Feast
77	Ten Hour Braised Beef Short Ribs — Janos
85	Tomatoes Concasse with Italian Sausage and Black Mussels — Jonathan's
137	Traditional Chicken Cacciatore — Mama Louisa's
33	Twice-Cooked Prime Rib — CuVée
123	White Chicken Enchiladas — Dakota Café

Desserts

141	Almendrado — Papagayo's
87	Almond Tuile Cookies — Jonathan's
103	Apple Crepes with Melted Brie — Pastiche
139	Capriotata — Miguel's
129	Chai Crème Brûlée — Intermezzo
57	Chocolate-Espresso Torte — Fuego
41	Chocolate Pots de Crème — Elle
21	Chocolate Wafer Cookies — Bistro Zin
57	Crème Brûlée — Fuego
45	Flambé of Stone Fruits with Ice Cream — Feast
145	Fresh Strawberries with Balsamic Vinegar — Roma Caffé
95	Limoncello Sorbet — Kingfisher
75	Napoleon of Strawberries and Grand Marnier Cream — Janos
95	Pecan Crusted Goat Cheese and Mascarpone Tarts — Kingfisher
47	Raspberry Tart with Dark Chocolate Ganache — Feast
81	Watermelon Granitée — Jonathan's
97	White Chocolate Whipped Cream Mousse — Kingfisher

Participating Restaurants

The following restaurants participated in the Primavera Cooks! events to benefit The Primavera Foundation. Here are their stories, menus and recipes.

This French-inspired American bistro has been one of Tucson's chic
eateries since it opened in June 2000. From day one, diners have packed
into the intimate red-walled quarters, where tables abut and you may
find yourself elbow-to-elbow with your neighbors. Music is lively and
the restaurant has a trendy buzz. Bistro Zin is located in a collection
of fashionable boutiques and restaurants.

Bistro Zin

ZIN BISTRO

Bistro Zin

1865 E River Road
299-7799
Serving Lunch, Dinner,
Late Night
$$$

Bistro Zin's appeal has always been twofold: food and fashion. With its extensive wine bar serving more than 60 varieties and its ever-changing French-inspired menu, the restaurant has nurtured a reputation as one of Tucson's best places to wine and dine. Bistro Zin, one of Sam Fox's celebrated upscale restaurants, presents inspired dishes that draw upon classic French cooking with a decidedly American twist. Here, a thin slice of silky foie gras sitting atop a crostini covered with Roquefort cheese serves as a warm-up to grilled ahi so fresh you expect it to flap its fins. Dishes change with the seasons and ingredients are dictated by what's fresh at the moment. There are some favorites that you can always find.

One thing sure not to change is the vast array of wines displayed in a cuvee and served by the glass or in "flights", a tasting of three related wines from different vintners. The restaurant has been given the prestigious Wine Spectator Award of Excellence each year from 2002 through 2005.

Sam Fox, whose Tucson-born restaurant empire now boasts several casual and fine-dining eateries in Tucson, Phoenix and Colorado, was one of the original Tucson Originals. There has been a Cooks! Event at Bistro Zin since 2003 and it is a restaurant that apprentices chose to return to year after year. Sam Fox supports Primavera Cooks! as a way to give back to the community and to showcase the talents of his team, led by Executive Chef Clinton Woods.

Bistro Zin
June 2003

EXECUTIVE CHEF

Clint Woods

APPRENTICE CHEFS

Shannon McBride-Olson
Steve Pageau
Ann Stevens

*"Chef Clint is a creative and
daring chef and an excellent teacher."*
~Shannon McBride-Olson

"It was a lot of work and a lot of fun."
~Steve Pageau

Hand Passed Canapés Osetra Caviar and Crème Fraîche Dungeness
Crab and Mango Salad, Escargot in Bouchée, Vegetable Gyozas •
Paul Chamblain Brut Blanc de Blancs

First Course Seared Big Eye Tuna, Melon Carpaccio, Radish
and Cucumber Consommé • Rihaku Wandering Poet

Second Course Warm Spinach Salad with Candied Pecans, Roasted
Peppers and Balsamic Glazed Shallots • Oxford Landing
Chardonnay

Third Course Rabbit Confit and Stone Fruit Napoleon, Mustard
Demi-Glaze and Crisp Wonton • Ravenswood Lodi Zinfandel

Fourth Course Australian Beef Tenderloin, Salsify Gratinée,
Wild Mushrooms • Foie Gras Jus de Veau

Fifth Course Primavera "Bars of Sin"

Left to right: Shannon McBride-Olson, Ann Stevens, Clint Woods,
and Steve Pageau

Salsify Gratinée and Mustard Demi-Glace

INGREDIENTS

Salsify Gratinée
3 large salsify roots
5 large potatoes
heavy cream
salt and white pepper

Mustard Demi-Glace
rabbit carcasses
chopped mirepoix, desired amount
sachet garni, desired amount
chicken stock
white wine
veal stock
Dijon mustard to taste
salt and pepper

For Salsify Gratinée Peel salsify and potatoes, slice on mandoline to ⅛ inch thickness and place in a greased pan. Toss in heavy cream, add just enough cream to cover the roots and potatoes. Season with salt and pepper. Bake uncovered in oven at 350° until golden brown.

For Mustard Demi-Glace Roast carcasses and mirepoix until golden brown. Deglaze pan with white wine. Add sachet and cover with half chicken and half veal stock. Strain stock, reduce nape. Add mustard and salt and pepper to taste. Use as a sauce.

Chocolate Wafer Cookies

INGREDIENTS

Chocolate Wafer Cookies
6 ounces butter, at room temperature
1 cup granulated sugar
1 large egg
1½ teaspoons vanilla extract
pinch of Kosher salt
⅔ cup dark cocoa powder sifted
1¼ cup all purpose flour

Preheat oven to 300°. Cream together sugar and butter until light and fluffy. Scrape down and add egg—mix to incorporate. Add vanilla, salt and gradually add sifted cocoa powder and flour. Mix to combine. Remove dough to a flat surface covered with parchment paper and flatten by hand. Put another layer of parchment on top of the dough and roll out to approximately ⅛" thickness. Chill for one hour until firm. Cut into desired shapes and prick with fork before baking. Bake for 8-10 minutes.

Bistro Zin
August 2004, Featuring Chalone Wine Group

EXECUTIVE CHEF

Clint Woods

APPRENTICE CHEFS

Bonnie Kohn
Olivia Sethi
Hank Schweighardt
Ann Stevens

"I did it last year and I want to do it again next year." ~Olivia Sethi

"Now I can appreciate all the hard work Chef Clint actually does—and keeps his sense of humor." ~Hank Schweighardt

First Course Amuse-Bouche, Cucumber Carpaccio, Poached Lump Crab and Sea Urchin Vinaigrette • Echelon Pinot Grigio

Second Course Charred Lobster Consomme, Heirloom Tomato Cannelloni and Micro Arugula • Edna Valley Chardonnay

Third Course Crispy Duck Breast with Petite Beet Salad and Fig Jus de Poulet • Chalone Pinot Noir

Fourth Course Mustard Crusted Lamb Chop with Root Vegetable Ratatouille and Wild Mushrooms • Sagelands Merlot

Fifth Course Frozen Hazelnut Soufflé, Peanut Butter Chocolate Truffles and Fresh Raspberries

Left to right: Olivia Sethi, Ann Stevens, Clint Woods, Bonnie Kohn, and Hank Schweighardt

Crispy Duck Breast with Fig Jus de Poulet

INGREDIENTS

Crispy Duck Breast

2, 6-7 ounce duck breasts

Fig Jus de Poulet

1 medium carrot, chopped

1 medium onion, chopped

2 ribs celery, chopped

1 bulb fennel, chopped

3 pounds roasted chicken bones

1 pound roasted duck bones

4 whole garlic cloves

2 sprigs fresh thyme

8-10 black peppercorns

2 bay leaves

½ cup sugar

4 quarts chicken stock

3 tablespoons unsalted butter

1 cup fresh black figs, cut into quarters

Kosher salt

fresh ground pepper

For Duck In warm sauté pan or on a preheated grill, place duck breasts fat side down. Cook the breast slowly to release the fat on breast (pouring it off as it cooks if you are using a sauté pan). Cook for 15 minutes or until brown and crisp.

For Fig Jus Preheat oven to 350°. Place chicken and duck bones on a cookie sheet and roast for about 10 minutes or until the bones are just past golden brown. In large saucepot, with oil, sauté together carrot, onion, celery and fennel until onion is translucent. Add to the onion mixture bones, garlic, thyme, peppercorns, bay leaves, sugar and chicken stock. Bring to a slow simmer and let cook for 2 hours. Remove from stove and pour the mixture through a fine strainer. Return the remaining liquid to a clean saucepan. Bring to a hard simmer and let cook until liquid is reduced by half leaving a rich stock. Allow to cool for ten minutes before folding in the butter, figs and salt and pepper. Set aside.

Plating Place each duck breast on a dinner plate, top with ¼ cup of the fig jus. Serve with a portion of the warm beet salad.

Petite Beet Salad

INGREDIENTS

Petite Beet Salad

½ pound whole baby stripped beets,
    washed with skins left on

½ pound whole golden baby beets,
    washed with skins left on

2 tablespoons extra virgin olive oil

Kosher salt and fresh ground pepper

fresh thyme, basil, and parsley

Preheat oven to 350°. Keeping the beets separate so that the red and golden beets do not discolor one another, season them with olive oil, salt and pepper and place into 2 separate roasting pans. Roast for 30 minutes. When cooked, peel and quarter beets. Toss with fresh thyme, basil and parsley. Season to taste with salt and pepper. Serve warm.

Bistro Zin August 2005

EXECUTIVE CHEF

Clint Woods

APPRENTICE CHEFS

Brad Geller
Werner Kroebig
Richard Weeks

*"So many varied dishes are created
from such a small selection of
ingredients and cooking equipment."
~Werner Kroebig*

*"I learned a trick to keep sugar from
crystallizing when making syrup."
~Richard Weeks*

First Course **Balsamic Marinated Rosemary Threaded Satay,
Scorched Bluefin Tuna, Organic Cucumber, Blood Orange
Gelee, and Micro Wasabi, Petite Vegetable Spring Roll,
Spicy Tamarind Glaze, Daikon Sprouts • Chateau De
Montfort Vouvray**

Second Course **Fresh Maine Lobster Soup with Sunizona Squash
Blossoms, Wild Morels, and Tiny Red Currant Tomato •
Caymus Conundrum**

Third Course **Herb Crusted Medallions of Colorado Lamb, Roasted
Cipollini Succotash, Minted-mustard Vinaigrette • Bogle Old
Vine Zinfandel**

Fourth Course **A Delectable Selection of Chocolate Delights •
Moon Mountain Cabernet Sauvignon**

Werner Kroebig

Left to right: Richard Weeks and Brad Geller

Seared Tuna Canapé

INGREDIENTS

Tuna Canapé

3 sheets gelatin

2 blood oranges

½ tablespoon fresh lemon juice

1 cup orange juice

½ tablespoon sugar

4 ounces bluefin tuna

½ teaspoon peanut oil

1 European cucumber

½ cup micro wasabi

Soak the gelatin sheets in ice water until soft (approximately three minutes). Press the blood oranges and strain through chinois. Add the fresh lemon juice, orange juice, and granulated sugar to the blood orange juice. In a medium saucepot, bring the ingredients to a simmer and reduce by ⅓. Remove from heat and using a spatula fold the gelatin sheets with the blood orange reduction (do not whip) and pour into 2 quart bowl and let cool. When cooled, dice the gelée.

In hot sauté pan, sear tuna in peanut oil until cooked to desired temperature (recommended served rare). Slice tuna ⅛ inch thick. Slice cucumbers ¼ inch thick. Place sliced tuna on sliced cucumber rounds. Place ¼ tsp of diced gelée and a couple sprigs of micro wasabi on top of the tuna to finish the canapé.

Chicken Satay

INGREDIENTS

Chicken Satay

2, 4-ounce chicken breasts

14 rosemary sprigs, 5-6" long

1 tablespoon parsley, chopped

1 tablespoon basil, chopped

1 tablespoon rosemary, chopped

½ cup olive oil

salt and pepper

Slice the chicken breasts on a bias creating strips 2 ½-3 inches long. Remove most of the rosemary leaves from the sprigs leaving a small amount on one end to hold onto. Reserve leaves for marinade. Skewer the chicken breast with the rosemary sprig. Place in a shallow pan. Mix the parsley, basil, and rosemary leaves together with olive oil and pour over chicken. Marinate for two hours. Grill until cooked through. Salt and pepper to taste and serve warm.

*Chef/owner Mitch Levy took a big chance in June 2003 when he opened
CuVée World Bistro. Most of the city's winter visitors were long gone,
and the long, hot, slow summer was in full swing. Tucson restaurant owners
dread that time of year, but Levy wasn't nervous. He didn't want his to be
a restaurant that catered to and depended upon winter residents for success.
He wanted to become a neighborhood bistro that folks would want to return
over and over again, no matter the time of year.*

CuVée World Bistro

CuVée World Bistro

3352 E Speedway
881-7577
Serving Lunch, Dinner,
Late Night
Closed Sunday
$$$

Mitch Levy, who grew up in Tucson, started cooking as a kid. His first true restaurant job was at a Jack-in-the-Box. He only lasted a month. Fortunately, he went on to graduate from the Western Culinary Institute in Portland, Oregon and spent several years working at resorts in Aspen, Colorado, before coming home to strike out on his own. He was well prepared.

Levy is happy to proclaim he has succeeded. CuVée is a comfortable, attractive restaurant with a reputation for exquisite fare that borrows equally from Southwestern, Italian and Pacific Rim cuisines. Each menu item is paired with an equally exquisite wine that may be ordered if desired: Crispy Calamari paired with a Sauvignon Blanc, Expensive Mushrooms Three Ways paired with a Pinot Noir, Mahogany Roasted Duck with a French red wine, Crème Brûlée with fresh berries paired with a Zinfandel. CuVée is becoming more of a true wine restaurant, with more wine pairings and wine dinners "We want to keep heading in that direction and do more wine dinners and those types of things," Levy says. This is possible logistically, because the restaurant has a very attractive special events space. "I want to stay with the times, but I don't want to change too much."

A month after opening CuVée, Levy volunteered to host a Primavera Cooks! Apprentice dinner. He has continued this every year. "It's such a great charity and it's such a fun event for everybody." says Levy. He likes the challenge of working with novice apprentices who have never before worked in a professional kitchen. He enjoys setting them free to create and they do: Crisp Gorgonzola Gnocchis with wild mushrooms and Panchetta in a Cabernet dressing, or Fresh Fruit and Berry Gazpacho with Late Harvest Zinfandel Granite.

CuVée World Bistro
August 2003

EXECUTIVE CHEF

Mitch Levy

APPRENTICE CHEFS

Mary Goethals
Curtis Lueck
Glenn Marks
Karla Weeks

First Course Shrimp and Calamari Ceviche with Roasted Tomatoes and Blue Corn Crisps • Brancott Sauvignon Blanc

Second Course Crisp Gorgonzola Gnocchis with Wild Mushrooms and Pancetta in a Cabernet Dressing • Cousino Macul Cabernet Sauvignon

Third Course New Castle Braised Lamb Shanks with Red Onion Confit and Yellow Pepper Orzo • Hollywood Red Cuvee

Fourth Course Fresh Fruit and Berry Gazpacho with Late Harvest Zinfandel Granite • Castoro Cellars Late Harvest Zinfandel

"The biggest compliment was seeing the empty plates come back to the kitchen." ~Curtis Lueck

"The slicing and dicing demonstration by the chefs was impressive."
~Mary Goethals

Top left photo: Mary Goethals
Left to right: Mitch Levy, Bob Petersen, Curtis Lueck, Mike Stefanowicz, Glenn Marks, Karla Weeks, and Dan Bradley

Gorgonzola Gnocchi Salad

INGREDIENTS

Gnocchi

1 tablespoon melted butter
⅛ cup heavy cream
1 cup gorgonzola
3 eggs
2½ cups all purpose flour
Kosher salt, to taste
black pepper, to taste

Salad

1 cup field greens
1 tablespoon olive oil
½ tablespoon garlic, chopped
½ tablespoon shallots, chopped
¼ cup mushrooms, sliced
⅛ cup cooked pancetta
¼ cup Cousino Macul
    Cabernet Sauvignon
Kosher salt
black pepper
gnocchi, prepared and sautéed

For Gnocchi Combine all of the ingredients in a mixing bowl and mix with hands until just incorporated. Do not overwork the dough or it will become tough. Roll a small portion of the dough into a "snake" and cut into uniform sized pieces. Using your thumb, press each piece into the back of a grater to give the gnocchi a hollow back and textured front. Place the gnocchi in a pot of boiling water and boil until they float. Remove from water and shock. Sauté the gnocchi in butter and oil until crisp and warm through.

For Salad In a hot sauté pan, sauté the garlic and shallots in the olive oil. Add the mushrooms and pancetta and sauté until mushrooms are soft. Deglaze with the wine and reduce by ½. Season to taste with the salt and pepper and toss with the greens. Place on the plate and garnish with the gnocchis. Eat um up, yum.

CuVée World Bistro July 2004

EXECUTIVE CHEF

Mitch Levy

APPRENTICE CHEFS

Joe Blair
Bill Blair
Fran Emrick
Lisa Lovallo

*"Chef Bob shared his nuances to
consistently turn out good bread and
delicious deserts." ~Fran Emrick*

*"Great cause and great time—and
I learned what a wonderful, caring
community of restaurateurs we have
in Tucson." ~ Lisa Lovallo*

First Course Grilled Summer Vegetable Tower with Marinated
Shrimp and Parmesan Tuilles • De Loach Viognier

Second Course Carpaccio of Venison with a Spicy Green Salad
in a Blackberry Zinfandel Dressing • De Loach Zinfandel

Third Course Crispy Seared Salmon over Caramelized Fennel
and White Bean Ragout with Spinach Purée and Fresh Herb
Chimichurry • De Loach Pinot Noir

Fourth Course Caramelized Tropical Fruit Melange over Vanilla
Bean Bavarian with Mango Coulis • De Loach Late Harvest
Gewürztraminer

Left to right: Mitch Levy, Bill Blair, Lisa Lovallo, Fran Emrick, Joe Blair,
and Bob Petersen

Carpaccio of Venison

INGREDIENTS

Venison

1 pound venison sirloin

1 tablespoon garlic, chopped

2 tablespoons olive oil

a sprinkle of Kosher salt

black pepper to taste

Rub the loin with all of the ingredients and mark on a hot grill, on all sides. Just cook enough to sear the outside, leaving the center raw. Let cool. Wrap tightly in plastic wrap then foil and freeze for 30 minutes until the outer ¼ inch is solid. Remove from foil and plastic and using a very sharp knife, slice the venison paper thin and place on the plate. This can be done ahead of time, cover with plastic in the fridge.

Blackberry Zinfandel Dressing

INGREDIENTS

Dressing

1 tablespoon olive oil

1 tablespoon garlic, chopped

1 tablespoon shallots, chopped

2 cups Zinfandel

4 tablespoons whole butter

1 pint blackberries

Kosher salt

black pepper

In a hot saucepot, sauté the garlic and shallots in the olive oil. Deglaze with the Zinfandel. Reduce to ⅓ cup of liquid. Once reduced, while constantly whipping, add the butter to the boiling mixture. When the butter is incorporated, add the blackberries and season to taste with the salt and pepper. Toss the dressing over the prepared greens and serve immediately. This dressing must be made just prior to serving; it will not hold for very long. Serve on selected spicy greens.

CuVée World Bistro
July 2005

EXECUTIVE CHEF

Mitch Levy

APPRENTICE CHEFS

Bill Blair
Vicki Nash

"This was as much fun as last year."
~Bill Blair

"I eat, live and breathe food and
I loved working and learning with
professional chefs." ~Vicki Nash

First Course Grilled Salmon Croustades with Fresh Apple Salsa • Greg Norman Sparkling Chardonnay

Second Course Fresh Spinach Salad with Candy Spiced Walnuts, Chevre and Dried Blueberry Dressing • Chateau St. Jean Fumé Blanc

Third Course Twice-Cooked Beef Ribeye with Twice Baked Cambazola Potatoes and Lavender Ratatouille in a Berringer Au Jus • Beringer Cabernet Sauvignon

Fourth Course Fresh Blueberry Soufflé Glacé with Port Reduction • Beringer Ruby Port

Left to right: Vicki Nash, Bob Petersen, Mitch Levy, and Bill Blair

Twice-Cooked Beef Ribeye

INGREDIENTS

Beef Ribeye

1 each, boneless prime rib
½ cup Kosher salt
½ cup garlic cloves
1 tablespoon liquid smoke
½ cup coarse black pepper
1 cup garlic, chopped
1 quart onions, cut rough
1 pint carrots, cut rough
1 pint celery, cut rough
olive oil
salt and pepper

Mix the salt with the liquid smoke. Rub the prime rib with oil, the garlic and salt and pepper. In a hot braising pan, sear all sides of the prime rib well. Place over the vegetables and roast in a 350° oven for one hour. Remove from oven and let cool. Slice into steaks and finish cooking them on the grill.

Cabernet Jus

INGREDIENTS

Cabernet Jus

½ cup roasted garlic
2 tablespoons shallots, chopped
2 tablespoon olive oil
1 quart Cabernet Sauvignon
2 cups veal stock or demi-glace
pan drippings from prime rib

In a hot sauce pot, sauté the roasted garlic and the shallots in the olive oil. Deglaze with the Cabernet and reduce by ½. Add the veal stock and drippings and simmer for 1 hour. Season to taste with Kosher salt and black pepper.

Self–professed foodie Jeff Fuld is the latest chef to take up residence in this celebrated corner spot of the historic Broadway Village, which is credited with being the oldest shopping center in Arizona. The attractive building, designed in 1939 by Josias Joesler, has housed a restaurant since the 1980s. Fuld ,who previously owned and operated Daniels in the Foothills, took over Elle last year. The venture allows Fuld, a wine connoisseur, to combine his love for food and vino.

Elle, a wine
country restaurant

elle
a wine country restaurant

Elle, a wine country restaurant

3048 E Broadway
327-0500
Serving Lunch and Dinner
$$-$$$

Jeff Fuld was in no rush to jump in and reshuffle the culinary deck at Elle. The restaurant already boasted a solid customer base because of its high quality wine country fare. Fuld jokes that some fans of Chef de Cuisine Antonio Cardadeiro's hugely popular Squash Ravioli with Spinach, Mushrooms and Sage Butter threatened a revolt if he tampered with the dish. "That's the one thing I was told not to take off the menu," Fuld said with a chuckle.

While he made no wholesale changes, Fuld did tweak things a bit to his liking. He decide to wrap the Brie appetizer in a flaky puffed pasty with chunks of walnuts and a cream sauce tart with cherries and a touch of Dijon, and put the shrimp ceviche in hollowed-out tomatoes with a spike of ginger that lends an amazing freshness. He added his fingerprints to the popular house gnocchi by topping the feather-light potato dumplings with a delicate mozzarella, a garlicky pesto and a tomato-based sauce kissed with cream.

Elle's menu will change with the seasons, with heartier offerings in colder weather. This winter, Fuld will re-introduce the lamb shank, one of his signature dishes, so tender it barely clings to the bone, served with a rich red wine sauce on a bed of creamy polenta.

Fuld plans to continue Elle's tradition of involvement in the Primavera Cooks! Event. "I've always believed in trying to give back and support the community,' he said, something he did at Daniels, as well. "That's what's nice about Tucson, especially with the independent restaurants; they give back to the community."

Elle, a wine country restaurant
September 2003

EXECUTIVE CHEF

Rich Koby

APPRENTICE CHEFS

Jean Paul Bierny
Tom Howayeck
Barbara Rosensimon
Chris Tanz

First Course Willcox Tomatoes, Fresh Mozzarella and Basil •
Ruffino Orvietto Classico

Second Course Cioppino with Baked Clams, Dungeness Crab Cake
and Grilled Sea Bass • Liberty School Syrah

Third Course Tuna Tataki with a Mushroom Napoleon, Texas
Tarragon Pesto • Whitehaven Pinot Noir

Fourth Course Molten Chocolate Cake with Mixed Berry Sauce

"It is amazing what can be accom-
plished in a small, very hot kitchen."
~Chris Tanz and Jean Paul Bierny

" I wanted to see what it would be like
to be a professional chef."
~Barbara Rosensimon

Left to right: Rich Koby, Jean Paul Bierny, Tom Howayeck, Barbara Rosensimon,
and Chris Tanz

Steamed Mussels with White Wine, Garlic and Herbs

INGREDIENTS

Steamed Mussels

2 pounds black mussels

2 tablespoons olive oil

1 shallot, finely minced

2 cloves garlic, finely minced

4 ounces dry white wine

4 ounces clear fish stock

1 tablespoon Italian parsley, chopped

½ tablespoon basil, chopped

½ tablespoon oregano, chopped

2 green onions, minced

1 tablespoon unsalted butter

½ cup diced tomato

Kosher salt

black ground pepper

In a saucepan, heat the olive oil with the shallots and garlic. Add the mussels, white wine, fish stock and herbs. Bring to a boil and cover, cook the mussels till they all open. Remove lid and finish with green onions, butter, and tomato. Salt and pepper to taste. Serve immediately.

Spinach Salad with Apple, Blue Cheese, and Walnuts with Sherry Vinaigrette

INGREDIENTS

Spinach Salad

½ pound baby spinach, picked and washed

2 tart apples, cored and thinly sliced

⅓ cup walnuts, toasted

2–3 ounces of your favorite blue cheese vinaigrette

1 shallot, finely minced

4 ounces olive oil

Kosher salt

black ground pepper

Sherry Vinaigrette

2 ounces sherry vinegar

1 ounce sherry

For Vinaigrette In a mixing bowl, add vinegar, sherry wine and shallots, slowly whisk in the olive oil. Season with salt and pepper to taste.

For Salad In a large bowl mix the spinach, walnuts, sliced apple and blue cheese. Dress the greens mixture with vinaigrette and serve immediately.

Elle, a wine country restaurant
September 2004

EXECUTIVE CHEF

Rich Koby

APPRENTICE CHEFS

Jennifer English
Jeff Grubic
Joe Heller
Hilary Peterson
Tom Wilson

"It reinforced my belief that I can't do this for a living." ~Joe Heller

"We had a blast. This is a unique fundraiser not just another typical charity dinner."
~Hilary Peterson and Tom Wilson

First Course **Shrimp and Goat Cheese Tamale with Arugula and Fruit Salsa** • Angeline Russian River Valley Chardonnay

Second Course **Seared Wild King Salmon with Roasted Vegetable Lasagna** • Eola Hills Pinot Noir

Third Course **Grilled Lamb Rack Chops with Herbed Risotto, Red Wine Butter Sauce** • Michel Schlumberger Maison Rouge

Fourth Course **Dark Chocolate Mousse with Espresso Crisp and Lingonberries** • Michael and David Phillips Lodi Earthquake Zinfandel

Left to right: Jennifer English, Hilary Peterson, Jeff Grubic, Tom Wilson, and Joe Heller

Grilled Lamb Chops with Herbed Risotto and Red Wine Butter Sauce

INGREDIENTS

Lamb Chops, Risotto and Butter Sauce

2, 8 bone lamb racks

3 cups risotto, prepared

1 tablespoon chopped parsley

2 tablespoons chopped rosemary

1¼ cup of grated Parmesan

1 pound unsalted butter

2 cups red wine

1 tablespoons red wine vinegar

1 shallot, roughly chopped

2 tablespoons whole black peppercorns

1 bay leaf and sprig of thyme

6 parsley stems

½ cup heavy cream

salt and pepper

olive oil

For Risotto Fold in the chopped parsley and rosemary into prepared risotto with salt and pepper. Fold in Parmesan and ¼ cup butter. Set aside and keep warm.

For Sauce In heavy saucepan, add red wine, vinegar, shallot, black peppercorns, bay leaf, thyme and parsley stems. Reduce over high heat until almost dry. Add heavy cream and reduce by ¾. Reduce heat to medium and slowly whisk in the remaining butter. Strain and season with salt and pepper to taste and reserve.

For Lamb Chops Cut lamb racks into individual chops. Preheat grill on high. Lightly oil chops and season with salt and pepper. Place chops on grill and cook to desired doneness.

Plating Place ½ cup of risotto in center of plate. Lean 2 lamb chops against risotto crossing the bones at the top. Drizzle 1 to 2 ounces of butter sauce over lamb chops and garnish with rosemary sprig.

Seared Salmon with Roasted Vegetable Lasagna

INGREDIENTS

Salmon with Lasagna

6, 4-ounce salmon fillets

2 cups béchamel sauce

4 8x8 sheets of fresh pasta

1 pint button mushrooms,
    quartered and roasted

1 cup Parmesan, grated

2 yellow squash, diced and roasted

2 zucchini, diced and roasted

olive oil

salt and pepper

parsley, chopped

For Lasagna Preheat oven to 350°. Grease an 8x8 baking pan. Place one sheet of pasta in pan and cover with 1 cup of béchamel sauce. Add layer of mushrooms and ⅓ of the grated Parmesan. Add another layer of pasta and cover with 1 cup of béchamel. Add a layer of yellow squash and ⅓ of the grated Parmesan. Add another layer of pasta and cover with the final cup of béchamel. Add zucchini and remaining Parmesan. Cover with last sheet of pasta and coat top with olive oil. Cover pan with foil. Bake 45 minutes.

For Salmon Heat a heavy sauté pan over high heat. Add 2 tablespoons olive oil. Season salmon with salt and pepper and place in pan. Sear 3 minutes on each side and remove from pan.

To Serve Cut lasagna into 6 pieces. Put a piece of lasagna in center of the plate. Place salmon on top of lasagna. Garnish with parsley.

Elle, a wine country restaurant
August 2005

EXECUTIVE CHEFS

Tony Cardadeiro
Jeff Fuld

APPRENTICE CHEFS

Shelly Gallichio
Keith Lierman
Cynthia McFarlin
Chuck Nickel

*"I appreciate the way Primavera
deals with the source of the problem,
not just the symptoms."*
~Cynthia McFarlin

*"Everything is so much bigger—
the pots, the bowls and utensils
and the quantity of spices."*
~Shelly Gallichio

First Course Chilled Scallop Mousse with Citrus-Rock Shrimp Stuffing and Green Apple Aioli • MacMurray Pinot Gris

Second Course Smoked Tomato Bisque • McWilliams Chardonnay

Third Course Orecchiette Pasta with Chicken and Roasted Garlic Sausage, Roasted Mushrooms and Grilled Eggplant • Da Vinci Chianti Classico

Fourth Course Slow Roasted Leg of Lamb stuffed with Roasted Peppers, Basil and Pine Nuts served over Saffron Couscous with Roasted Fennel • Louis Martini "Alexander Valley" Cabernet Sauvignon

Fifth Course Chocolate Pots de Crème • Louis Martini "Gnarly Vines" Zinfandel

Left to right: Cynthia McFarlin, Shelly Gallichio, Keith Lierman, Jeff Fuld, Tony Cardadeiro and Chuck Nickel

Orecchiette Pasta with Chicken and Roasted Garlic Sausage, Mushrooms and Eggplant

INGREDIENTS

Chicken and Roasted Sausage

3⅓ pounds boneless, skinless chicken
    breast, diced
⅔ pounds yellow onion, diced
⅓ pounds unsalted butter
1 teaspoon each sage, thyme, celery salt
1 teaspoon black pepper
⅔ ounce Kosher salt
1 cup roasted garlic cloves
½ cup finely chopped carrots

Orecchiette

6 cups orecchiette, prepared al dente
1 teaspoon each chopped garlic and shallots
1 tablespoons olive oil
2 pounds chicken/roasted garlic sausage
1 pint button mushrooms quartered/roasted
1 eggplant peeled, grilled, cut into batonets
¼ cup dry white wine
1 cup heavy cream
salt and pepper
Parmesean, grated
parsley, chopped

For Sausage Sweat onions in butter until translucent. Add onions, butter and remaining ingredients into chicken. Mix thoroughly, grind through medium dye.

For Orecchiette In large sauté pan, sauté olive oil, garlic, shallots and sausage in sauté pan and cook until sausage is nearly completely cooked. Add mushrooms and eggplant and sauté 1 to 2 additional minutes. Add white wine and cook off. Add cream and simmer 1 minute. Season with salt and pepper. Toss with pasta, place in bowls and garnish with fresh grated Parmesan and chopped parsley.

Chocolate Pots de Crème

INGREDIENTS

Chocolate Pots de Crème
1 cup half and half
2 cups heavy cream
½ teaspoon vanilla extract
6 egg yolks
7 ounces dark chocolate melted
⅓ cup granulated sugar
whipped cream and cocoa powder

Preheat oven to 350°. Scald half and half, cream, vanilla, and half of granulated sugar. Temper into yolks and remaining sugar. Cool to body temperature. Whisk in melted chocolate. Skim foam and pour into custard dishes. Place custard dishes in a water bath and cover. Bake for 30 minutes checking periodically. Custards are done when center slightly moves when tapped. Remove from water and cool in refrigerator for at least 4 hours. Top each custard with dollop of whipped cream. Dust with cocoa powder and serve.

Restaurants are a lot like children: as they grow and mature, they sometimes outgrow their nicknames. That's what has happened to the 4-year-old Feast Tasteful Takeout. Now it's more "Feast" than "Takeout."

Feast
Restaurant

Feast Restaurant

4122 E Speedway
326-9363
Serving Lunch and Dinner
Closed Mondays
$$-$$$

Ever since Doug Levy knocked down a wall and expanded his restaurant from a 28-seater to a 60-seater, the term "takeout" no longer applies. Nor does it give justice to the gourmet meals served. In the smaller space, there was no room for wait staff to take orders tableside, so most orders were placed at the counter, and many of those orders marched out of the restaurant with the diners. The delicious "to go" food and extensive catering is still available. But now, in the enlarged space, wait staff bustles about filling water glasses, taking orders and delivering meals with wines from Feast's extensive wine list to a buzzing crowd.

Levy is quick to call his cuisine a "pretty eclectic mess," The menu maintains consistent favorites: Linguine alla Carboara, Roasted Pork Sandwich with Quince Paste and Asiago Cheese, Salmon Cakes, Strawberry Shortcake and Gingerbread. But, as Levy says, "We change the menu every month, so it's kind of an ever-changing multicultural menu." You can find a Mexican dish, Pork Picadillo, with a Thai dish, Curried Shrimp, during the same month. As he says, "It's fairly all over the place."

The constant menu change makes for orderly chaos of the finest, tastiest kind, where experimentation is encouraged and dishes can dance across the map — a recent four-layer salmon dish, for example, rested on a bed of mashed potatoes spiked with a Vietnamese chile sauce for an Asian "kiss." "It keeps us all excited about what we're doing, and I think you can taste the difference in a dish made by someone who's excited and a dish made by someone who's made it 20,000 times and is on autopilot," Levy said.

As soon as Levy opened Feast as owner/chef, he generously made it available for the annual Primavera Cooks! Apprentice Event. He feels "It's just a great event. There's such a tremendous spirit of community. We do a lot of charitable events, and they're all great causes, but what I really like about this event is that it's done on a smaller scale and you don't feel like you're milling around with 1,200 people, with everybody going from table to table getting appetizers." You're enjoying a dinner. "It's an intimate setting, and it allows you to meet new people."

Feast Restaurant
August 2002

EXECUTIVE CHEF

Doug Levy

APPRENTICE CHEFS

Shannon McBride-Olson
Ann Stevens
Dolores Zimmerman

First Course Lobster, Corn and Scallion Bread Pudding with Parmesan Vin Blanc • Mountain Dome Brut

Second Course Salad of Baby Greens with Fresh Basil, Mint and Jicama in a Sweet Citronette • Nautilus Sauvignon Blanc

Third Course Grilled Wild Colombia River Sturgeon, served over Carrot-simmered Israeli Couscous with Braised Belgian Endive, Pancetta and Lemon-Port Butter • Rutz Sonoma Coast Pinot Noir

Fourth Course Flambé of Stone Fruits with Vanilla Bean Ice Cream • Eola Hills "Vin d'or" Late Harvest Sauvignon Blanc

"This was a hobby cook's dream. Wild tigers couldn't prevent me from signing up again." ~Ann Stevens

"I am exhausted but happy." ~Dolores Zimmerman

Left to right: Shannon McBride-Olson, Dolores Zimmerman, and Ann Stevens

Lobster, Corn and Scallion Bread Pudding

INGREDIENTS

Bread Pudding

1 lobster

6 eggs, divided use

1, 1-pound baguette,
   cut into cubes

½ cup milk

2 cup cream

2 ears corn, kernel cut
   fresh from the cob

1 bunch scallions, chopped

4 tablespoons butter

Preheat oven to 350°. Grease 8, six-ounce ramekins. Boil the lobster, cool, shell and cut into ½ inch pieces. Separate two of the eggs, reserving both the yolks and the whites. In mixing bowl, beat the whites to stiff peaks and set aside. Toss the bread cubes with the milk, cream, yolks and remaining whole eggs. In a medium pan, sauté the corn and scallion in the butter until the corn just begins to soften. Mix the corn and scallions into the bread mixture. Fold in the whites. Spoon the mixture into the ramekins. Place the ramekins in a water bath. Bake for 20 minutes, turn, and bake for another 20 minutes. When the center of the puddings are as firm as the edges, remove from oven and let cool.

Flambé of Stone Fruits with Ice Cream

INGREDIENTS

Flambé

1 ripe peach, pitted
   and cut into eighths

1 ripe nectarine, pitted
   and cut into eighths

2 ripe plums, pitted
   and quartered

2 ripe apricots, pitted
   and quartered

1 dozen cherries, pitted

6 tablespoons butter

4 tablespoons sugar

6 tablespoons brandy

Over medium-high heat, sauté the fruit in half of the butter. Add the sugar right away, and once the granules have melted, add the brandy (be careful — it will ignite). Let the alcohol burn off and stir in the remaining butter. Serve over ice cream.

Feast Restaurant
September 2003

EXECUTIVE CHEF

Doug Levy

APPRENTICE CHEFS

Jimmy Crabb
Fran Emrick
Bonnie Kohn

First Course Timbale of Roast Vegetables and Chevre with Tomato Water and Fresh Basil • Westerly Sauvignon Blanc

Second Course Salad of Field Greens with Grapefruit Poppy Seed Dressing, Fresh Berries, Spiced Pecans and Chevre • Bodegas Bretón "Loriñon" Rioja Blanca

Third Course Spiced and Seared Ahi Tuna with Prosciutto Ham, Cantaloupe Sauce and Haricots Verts • Il Circo "La Violetta" Uva di Troia

Fourth Course Fresh Raspberry Tart with Dark Chocolate Ganache • Yalumba "D Black" Sparkling Cabernet/Shiraz

"I cook a lot and Doug was great to work with." ~Jimmy Crabb

"I'd like to do it next year too." ~Bonnie Kohn

Left to right: Jimmy Crabb, Bonnie Kohn, Doug Levy, and Fran Emrick

Grapefruit Poppy Seed Dressing

INGREDIENTS

Dressing

2½ cups grapefruit juice

½ cup rice wine vinegar

4 egg yolks

¼ cup each honey and sugar

2 cups each olive oil and corn oil

2 tablespoons poppy seeds

2 grapefruits, cut into imperials
    and minced

salt and pepper

In a food processor, blend the grapefruit juice, vinegar, egg yolks, honey and sugar until smooth. With the motor running, gradually add the oils until emulsified. Stir in the poppy seeds. Stir in grapefruit and season with salt and pepper to taste.

Raspberry Tart with Dark Chocolate Ganache

INGREDIENTS

Raspberry Tart

fresh raspberries

pâté sucrée

¼ cup flour

¼ teaspoon salt

1 tablespoon sugar

8 tablespoons or 1 stick
    unsalted butter, cold

1 egg, lightly beaten

ice water

Ganache

½ cup heavy cream

8 ounces dark chocolate,
    finely chopped

1 tablespoon butter

For tart Combine flour, salt and sugar in food processor and mix. Quarter butter lengthwise and cut into 8-9 pieces; scatter evenly over flour mixture. Pulse until butter pieces are the size of lentils. Place lightly beaten egg in ¼ cup measure and fill to top with ice water. Put half liquid in bottom of a bowl. Turn flour/butter mixture onto it pouring remaining liquid evenly over the top. Using a rubber spatula, fold mixture until evenly moistened. Squeeze; it should hold together. Sprinkle more water if needed. Put mixture on table and quickly fraiser (using palms of hand, push sections of dough away from you). Gather dough and fraiser missed portions. Form into desired shapes. Wrap in plastic. Chill at least 30 minutes or up to 3 days (freeze up to 3 months). Preheat oven to 350°. Roll out dough and fit into tart molds. Prick dough with fork, line tart shells with foil and fill with dry beans or pie weights. Bake until crust is set, about 10 minutes, remove weights and bake until golden brown, 10-15 minutes. Cool.

For Ganache In a medium pot, bring cream to a boil. In a mixing bowl pour it over the chocolate, whisking until smooth. Whisk in butter until dissolved. Pour mixture into tart shells and let cool. Top with fresh raspberries, chill and serve.

Feast Restaurant
June 2004

EXECUTIVE CHEF

Doug Levy

APPRENTICE CHEFS

Steve Pageau
Selene Waddell
Ann-Eve Pedersen

"I appreciated the way Doug could make the simplest dish seem elegant."
~Selene Waddell

"It was a lot of fun to step behind the scenes with Doug after having been on the receiving end of so many delicious meals at Feast."
~Ann-Eve Pedersen

First Course Spanish Chorizo and Seared Ahi Toasts with Fresh Herbs and Riesling Cream Asparagus and Chévre Phyllo Rolls • Mountain Dome Cuvée Forte

Second Course Stuffed Softshell Crab Stuffed Wrapped in Prosciutto over Salad of Frisée and Fresh Mint with Shallot Citronette and Mint Oil • Freie Weingärtner Wachau, Weissenkirchner Achleiten Riesling

Third Course Roast Game Hen with Cornbread Stuffing and Chipotle-Honey Glaze served over Calabacitas • Rosenblum 'Vintners Cuvée XXV' Zinfandel

Fourth Course Crème Brûlée with Fresh and Chocolate-Dipped Berries • Baumard, 'Clos de Sainte Catherine' Chenin Blanc

Left to right: Steve Pageau, Selene Waddell, Ann-Eve Pedersen, and Doug Levy

Stuffed Softshell Crabs Wrapped in Prosciutto over a Salad of Frisée and Fresh Mint with Shallot Citronette and Mint Oil

INGREDIENTS

Shallot Citronette

3 cloves garlic, minced

½ cup orange juice

½ cup lemon juice

½ cup lime juice

2 teaspoon honey

1 cup olive oil

2 shallots, chopped

salt and pepper

Mint Oil

¼ pound fresh mint

4 ounces grapeseed oil

salt and pepper

Softshell Crabs

olive oil

4 softshell crabs, cleaned and dressed

rice flour seasoned salt

pepper

2 paper-thin slices prosciutto ham,
    cut in half lengthwise

3 ounces Brie, cut into 4 equal pieces

2 heads frisée, cut and washed

2 ounces fresh mint leaves

2 ounces shallot citronette

mint oil

For Shallot Citronette Put the first 5 ingredients into a food processor. With the motor running, drizzle in the olive oil. Add the shallots and season with salt and pepper to taste.

For Mint Oil Pick the mint from the stems, reserving the stems. Over medium-low heat, simmer the mint stems in the oil for 15-20 minutes. Let the oil cool. Put the leaves in a food processor and gradually drizzle the grapeseed oil in with the motor running. Season with salt and pepper to taste.

For Softshell Crabs In a sauté pan, heat 2-3 tablespoons of olive oil over medium-high heat. In mixing bowl season rice flour with salt and pepper to taste. Dredge the crabs in flour mixture and sauté them to golden brown, about 1 ½ minutes on each side. Remove them from the pan and cut them in half with the legs sticking out on either side. Place a chunk of Brie between the two halves of each crab and wrap them with the prosciutto, with the legs sticking up and the cut side down. Set them back in the pan, removed from the heat, to keep them warm. Toss the frisée and mint with the citronette and set a tuft on each of four plates. Lean the crab bundles against the greens and garnish with mint oil.

Feast Restaurant
June 2005

EXECUTIVE CHEF

Doug Levy

APPRENTICE CHEFS

Ivy Schwartz
Olivia Sethi
Jeff Silvyn

First Course Crab-Manchego Custard with Basil Oil and Oven-Cured Tomatoes • Segura Viudas "Creu de Lavit" Xarel-lo

Second Course Mixed Greens in a Grapefruit Citronette with Toasted Pecan-Crusted Goat Cheese • Martinsancho Rueda Blanca

Third Course Braised Pork in a Sherried Tomato Broth with Caramelized Onions, Littleneck Clams and Fresh Spinach • Segura Viudas "Mas d' Aranyó" Tempranillo Reserva,

Fourth Course Molten Chocolate Cake with Fresh Bing Cherries • Olivares Dulce Monastrell

"We had a great time brainstorming to plan the meal with the benefit of Doug's insights on flavor, complementary styles and presentation."
~Jeff Silvyn

"Fast and furious and incredibly fun."
~Ivy Schwartz

Left to right: Ivy Schwartz, Olivia Sethi, Jeff Silvyn, Ken Steen, and Doug Levy

Braised Pork with Clams and Vegetables

INGREDIENTS

Braised Pork with Clams

3 pound boneless pork shoulder or
   butt rubbed with spice mix; wrap
   and let sit refrigerated overnight.
2 dozen littleneck clams,
   thoroughly washed

Cut into large pieces:

2 small carrots
2 ribs celery
1 large yellow onion
6 cloves whole peeled garlic

Add into pot:

8 cups chicken stock
2 cups dry sherry
1 teaspoon whole peppercorns
3 bay leaves
2 large tomatoes, quartered and roasted
½ pound shrimp shells (optional)
one bunch spinach

Spice Rub

1 tablespoon salt
6 tablespoons paprika
1 teaspoon cayenne
2 tablespoons powdered onion
2 tablespoons powdered garlic
½ teaspoon white pepper

In a large pot, sauté the vegetables in olive oil over high heat until they begin to soften. Add the pork and brown it evenly on all sides. Add remaining ingredients to pot except for the clams and spinach. Bring to a boil, reduce heat to a simmer and cook covered for four hours. Turn the pork over and simmer for two more hours. Thoroughly wash and add 2 dozen littleneck clams, check seasoning. The clams are quite salty and extra salt should not be required. The pork should pull apart into tender chunks and the clams should open by themselves. Add spinach, washed and stemmed. Serve the pork and clams over mashed potatoes or rice with the broth, stirring in 4 tablespoons unsalted butter if desired.

Glistening knotty-pine floors greet you at Fuego, the southwestern restaurant brainchild of Tucson celebrity chef Alan Zeman. Zeman, of course, blushes at the notion that he's a celebrity, but his résumé tells the tale: stints at private clubs, hotels and resorts, and his own gourmet products line marketed nationwide. He has appeared locally and nationally on television and was featured on the popular PBS series "Great Chefs." Zeman also hosts a local radio show, "The Z'Mans Restaurant Corner,"

Fuego Restaurant Bar & Grill

Fuego Restaurant Bar and Grill

6958 E Tanque Verde Road
886-1745
Serving Dinner
$$$

Alan Zeman's heart is focused on Fuego. Here diners can nibble soft charbroiled fish tacos dressed up with grilled peppers and onions and fresh avocado at a table near the brick fireplace, or contemplate the finer points of the grilled polenta or Prickly Pear Pork Tenderloin as they glance out a picture window that frames the majestic Santa Catalina Mountains.

Zeman, a graduate of the Culinary Institute of America, is famous for his flair and imagination in preparing a wide range of dishes. He features cuisine indigenous to the southwestern area of the United States and specializes in serving fresh seafood. Ostrich is a standard offering at Fuego and the Caesar Grande Salad features a roasted garlic bulb that brings out the true intentions of a Caesar salad.

Zeman will celebrate the restaurant's 10th anniversary in January 2006. The eatery, located on Tucson's east side, has an equally strong reputation as an entertainment destination, with its popular Sunday night program, Sinatra Sunday, featuring Frank Sinatra impersonator Paul Elia. As he contemplates the next 10 years, Zeman said he might expand the entertainment offerings.

Fuego has hosted the Primavera Cooks! Event for three years, and Zeman works with the apprentice chefs with the same professionalism — and good-natured ribbing — that he applies to his staff. "Cooks! is a great event. The apprentice chefs pay Primavera for the privilege of working in our kitchen and everybody really gets into it. There's a lot of enthusiasm and the apprentices have a great attitude."

Fuego Restaurant Bar and Grill
July 2003 South African Wine Dinner

EXECUTIVE CHEF

Alan Zeman

APPRENTICE CHEFS

Judy Dye
Shelly Gallichio
Melinda Kay

"This is hard work!" ~Judy Dye

"The pairing of wine varietals with food opened my eyes to the subtleties of flavor pairing." ~Melinda Kay

First Course "Whitsuntide"…"SnookTime" Hot Smoked Snook with Peach Atjar Cucumber Salad and Jumbo Caper Berries • Glen Carlou Chardonnay

Second Course "Sosaties" The Original Malay Dish and a South African Tradition Marinated Skewered Pork Grilled with Apricots and Apples atop "Vendusierys" Rice • Indaba Pinotage

Third Course "Forefathers Bobotie and Boerwors" with Sultana Chutney and "Slaphaksiceentjies" (Cooked Onion Salad) A Beef "Hot Dish" with Fresh Grilled Sausage • Mulderbosch Faithful Hound

Fourth Course "Triple A" Ostrich Sauté with a Field Mushroom Medley Cabernet Sauce and a "Brinjal" Dish (Eggplant, Tomatoes and Chilies) • Glen Carlou Grand Classique

Fifth Course "Mimie Zeeman" of Goudmyn's" Grape Tart with Tant, Nonnies' Buttermilk Custard and Koeksisters • Fuego Caliente Coffee

Left to right: Judy Dye, Alan Zeman, Shelly Gallichio, and Melinda Kay

Ostrich Sauté Cabernet

INGREDIENTS

Ostrich Sauté

8, 3-ounce prime muscle portions
   of ostrich
flour to dust
4 polenta rounds (recipe below)
4 ounces sliced Portobello mushrooms
1 ounce Cabernet wine
1 teaspoon chopped shallots
4 ounces Cabernet wine jelly
4 ounces glacé de viande

Wine Jelly

Cabernet wine jelly
1 bottle Cabernet wine
1½ cups sugar
2 ounces liquid pectin

For Ostrich Season and sear off polenta. In hot sauté pan, lightly flour, season, and sauté ostrich medallions. Turn, add mushrooms, sauté, deglaze with red wine and shallots. Remove meat from pan, add wine jelly and glacé and reduce until sauce is nicely thickened. Return meat to pan, simmer briefly in sauce. Arrange atop polenta with sauce, vegetable, and sweet potato chips.

For Jelly In stainless steel pan reduce sugar and wine by one half. Stir in pectin and cool. Yields one pint.

Polenta Rounds

INGREDIENTS

Polenta Rounds

3½ onions
2 cloves of garlic
1½ ounces fat
2½ cups water
2½ cups milk
½ ounce salt
8 ounces cornmeal,
   coarsely ground
3½ ounces Parmesan
   cheese, grated
1 pound butter

In medium pot, sauté onions and garlic in fat. Add water and milk, bring the mixture to a boil. Add salt. Gradually add the cornmeal and boil rapidly for 5 minutes, stirring constantly. Reduce heat and simmer for 90 minutes. Do not stir, a crust on the bottom of the pan is desirable. Before serving, add grated Parmesan cheese, or serve separately.

Fuego Restaurant Bar and Grill
July 2004

EXECUTIVE CHEF

Alan Zeman

APPRENTICE CHEFS

Lisa Abrams
Kristen Cook
Shelly Gallichio
Mark Kahlich

"I'm a big 'foodie' and I liked getting a behind-the scenes look at a real live kitchen." ~Kristen Cook

"I loved it and I loved that you could put your dirty dishes to the side and then they were clean." ~Shelly Gallichio

First Course Brucshetta Bar "A la Gallichio" Crostini Melted Mozzarella with a Bevy of Pestos and Toppings, Hot Smoked Salmon with Tomato Basil Salad, Capers and Creme Fraiche • Zenato Pinot Grigio

Second Course Kahlich's Crab, Crispy Cashew Crusted Soft Shell Crab with Pineapple Salsa, Cucumber Wrapped Summer Greens and a Drizzle of Miso Vinaigrette • Robert Mondavi Fume Blanc Napa Valley

Third Course "The Beak" Duxelle Stuffed Poussin and Ravioli with Crimini and Portobello Sauce, Fresh Sage and Sprinkle of Parmesan • Frescobaldi Castiglioni Chianti

Fourth Course Loin of Lamb "LA" Wrapped and Roasted in an Appareil of Spinach, Shallots and Herbs atop Farro Cake with Medley of Sugar Peas and Baby Carrots with Cabernet Wine Jelly Sauce • Robert Mondavi Oakville Cabernet Sauvignon

Fifth Course The Cook's Sampler: Chocolate Espresso Torte with Bananas Flambé, Wattleseed Creme Brûlée, Chocolate Dipped Strawberry and White Chocolate, Pistachio Chip Cookie • Woodbridge Porta Cinco 1995

Left to right: Lisa Abrams, Alan Zeman, Shelly Gallichio, Mark Kahlich, and Kristen Cook

Chocolate-Espresso Torte

INGREDIENTS

Torte

1 pound bittersweet, good-quality
    chocolate

zest of 1 orange

1 pound butter

9 ounces hot espresso or strong coffee

8 ounces (or 1 generous cup) sugar

6 large whole eggs

6 large egg yolks

whipped cream

Chop chocolate into fine pieces. Reserve in a bowl with orange zest. Bring butter, espresso and sugar to a boil. Pour over chocolate and stir until all chocolate is melted. Cool to room temperature. Whisk eggs and yolks in a bowl until combined and whisk in the chocolate mixture. Pour into a greased 9-inch cake pan that has been lined with parchment paper. (Do not use a springform pan). Place in a water bath; bake at 325° for 45 minutes to 1 hour until cake rises and cracks slightly. Cake will still jiggle and be loose in the center. Cool to room temperature. Cake will fall slightly. Turn out of pan and serve with whipped cream.

Crème Brûlée

INGREDIENTS

Crème Brûlée

2 quarts heavy cream

1 vanilla bean, split

2 cups sugar

3 whole eggs

15 egg yolks

additional sugar

In a saucepan, mix together the cream, vanilla bean and half of the sugar. Cook on stove until close to boiling. In mixing bowl, mix the eggs, yolks and remaining sugar together. Temper hot cream into egg mixture, stirring constantly. Strain through a fine-mesh strainer. Pour into ramekins; place in water bath, cover in plastic wrap and bake at 300° for about 1 hour. Check brûlées as they are baking to see if the oven is too hot or too cool. As soon as they are set, remove from oven and place on rack to cool. Before serving, sprinkle a light dusting of sugar across the top and heat with a kitchen torch until the sugar is caramelized and bubbly.

You can add flavorings such as ginger, fennel or star anise to the cream as it is cooking.

Fuego Restaurant Bar and Grill
August 2005

EXECUTIVE CHEF

Alan Zeman

APPRENTICE CHEFS

Kathy Dixon
Joe Heller
Dee Dee McCabe
Doug McClure

*"We worked very hard and
I loved every minute of it."
~Dee Dee McCabe*

*"I finally learned the proper way
to cook beets." ~Kathy Dixon*

First Course "Hosted" Hot-Smoked American Sturgeon with Apricot-Poblano Compote, "Iced" Flying Fish Caviar and Cold-Smoked British Columbia Salmon with Buckwheat Blinis, Capers, Chives and Sour Cream • Jekel Riesling

Second Course "Boasted" Crispy Sesame Fried Soft-Shell Crab with Shiitake Mushroom Salsa, Bean Sprouts, Sugar Peas and Mushroom Soy Beurre Blanc • Sonoma-Cutter, Chardonnay

Third Course "Posted" Peppercorn Duck Liver Pate, Bibb and Red Leaf Lettuces with Chevre, Candied Pistachios, Grilled Pear and Crostini • Five Rivers Pinot Noir

Fourth Course "Roasted" Ballotine of Roasted Duckling with Duck Confit Sausage, Golden Beets, Broccolini and Cannellini Beans • Bonterra Syrah

Fifth Course "Toasted" Caramelized Peach Tart with Brandy Snap, Berry and Peach Salsa Sabayon • Korbel Brut 'Natural'

Wines generously donated by Alliance Beverage and Brown-Forman.

Left to right: Joe Heller, Doug McClure, Dee Dee McCabe, Kathy Dixon, and Alan Zeman

Apricot Poblano Compote

INGREDIENTS

Apricot Poblano Compote

1 tablespoon shallots, chopped

1 tablespoon garlic, chopped

2 quarts dried apricots, diced

3, 5-ounce cans apple juice

1 cup cooking sake (Mirin)

1 tablespoon curry powder

3 Poblano chilies, roasted,
   peeled and diced

olive oil

Sweat shallot and garlic for 3 minutes in 1 tablespoon olive oil. Add apricots and cook an additional 5 minutes. Add apple juice, sake, and curry powder. Simmer until liquid is reduced by ¾. Add Poblano chiles and remove from heat.

Duck Confit

INGREDIENTS

Duck Confit Cure

1 pound Kosher salt

1 ounce curing salt

1 tablespoon ground star anise

1 teaspoon ground clove

2 teaspoons leaf thyme

8 each, duck leg and thigh quarters

duck fat (or oil)

Sprinkle raw duck legs with cure mixture on both sides. Let sit (cure) overnight. Rinse with cold water, pat dry. Cover with fat in earthenware covered container and bake at 300° for 2-3 hours or until meat is tender. Meat may be stored in fat for weeks. Pull meat, discarding bones and skin, dice and chill. May be used in suasage, salads or as a main dish. Be very careful handling hot fat...it may also be stored and reused.

Chef/owner Coralie Satta-Williams can't pinpoint what it is about her north side café that makes coming to work every day such a treat. "I absolutely love what I do," she says, then laughs in a way that is contagious. "I was in France for a month and I couldn't wait to get back to work. I love my staff. I love my customers." Satta-Williams learned her craft on the job, first with her father in his bakery and then under the tutelage of top chefs in her native France.

Ghini's French Caffe

Ghini's French Caffe

1803 E Prince Road
326-9095
Serving Breakfast and Lunch
Closed Mondays
$$-$$$

Satta-Williams was just 22 when she opened the restaurant in 1992, in a shopping plaza next door to her father's French bakery. She uses his breads on her sandwiches stuffed fat with yellowfin tuna salad, roasted deli meats and veggies. The sandwiches go from the ordinary — ham and cheese — to the extraordinary: hothouse tomatoes with garlic and more garlic highlight the Garlic Lover's; Brie cheese makes a fine substitute for the Gruyère on the Chicken Cordon Bleu; and top-of-the-line Spanish anchovies serve as a fine foundation for the Marseillaise.

It's not unusual for Satta-Williams, the mother of a young daughter, to clock in 12-hour days minding the store. Until last year, she divided her time between Ghini's and its sister café, located at the Northwest Medical Center. She sold the smaller restaurant and is now focusing her energy on Ghini's. She hopes to expand to allow for more private party functions by late 2005.

The menu likely won't undergo changes. It includes fields of fresh salads that include exquisite ingredients like homemade paté, organic baby spinach and yellowfin or ahi tuna. Breakfast is highlighted by omelets generously filled with bacon, cheese, veggies, potatoes, herbs and anchovies. The French side of the menu includes Eggs Provençal, an array of fresh crepes, traditional French baguettes with sweet cream butter, and classic French toast, served with fresh strawberry coulis and whipped cream or hot buttered apple rum. Recently, a complement of French wines, Pastis and imported beers have been added.

Satta-Williams hosted a Primavera Cooks lunch in 2002. "I think we had 30-35 people," she recalled. "It was a lot of fun. The best thing about being a member of the Tucson Originals is that we're constantly doing things for charities. And we do it wholeheartedly; it's not as a gimmick."

Ghini's French Caffe
September 2002

EXECUTIVE CHEF

Coralie Williams

APPRENTICE CHEFS

Lucy Mitchell
Fran Emrick

First Course Entreè Pâté de Campagne, Plat de Resistance, Sole Capres aux Olives en Papillote (Capered Sole with Olives in Parchment)

Second Course Garniture, Riz aux Poireaux (Vegetable Leek Rice Pilaf)

Third Course Course Salade de Mesclun Avec une Vinaigrette au Citron (Baby Mesclun with a Lemon Vinaigrette), Fromage Fermiers (An Assortment of French Country Cheeses)

Fourth Course Tartelette aux Fruits (Fresh fruit tartelettes) • Andre Lurton Chateau Bonnet • Champagne Paul Chamblain "Blancs de Blancs" Brut

"Intensely busy with instantly made decisions, but the food comes out consistently beautiful and delicious."
~Fran Emrick

"Master Pastry Chef Adrien was a treat to watch." ~Lucy Mitchell

Left to right: Fran Emrick, Lucy Mitchell, and Coralie Williams

Capered Sole with Olives in Parchment

INGREDIENTS

Capered Sole

7 ounces fresh Dover sole fillet
1 ounce capers, drained
1 ounce oil cured black olives
1 pinch salt
1 pinch black pepper
1 pinch mustard seeds
1 ounce julienned leeks
   (seated in extra virgin olive oil
   and a few ounces of fish stock)
1 ounce the best extra virgin
   olive oil you can find
2 ounces white wine
   (to be added just before baking)
parchment paper
baking twine

Place sole in the middle of a 16" square piece of parchment and add each item in above order. Tie the parchment like a present tightly and bake at 400° for 12 minutes. Be careful when serving as there may be some steam.

Pâté de Campagne

INGREDIENTS

Pâté

8 ounces uncooked cold
   bacon chopped
¼ cup bacon fat
1 teaspoon salt
1 teaspoon pepper
1½ teaspoons thyme
4 ounces chicken livers
6 ounces ground pork
3 ounces white wine
6 ounces half and half
6 ounces ground lamb
5 ounces half and half
1 whole egg
½ tablespoon flour

Place bacon, fat, salt, pepper and thyme in large food processor. Begin running food processor and don't turn off. Add liver, pork, wine and one ounce of half and half through chute. Turn food processor off and mix well with a spatula. Turn food processor on again and add lamb and remaining half and half. You may have to turn off and mix with a spatula frequently, especially when you add liquid. Add egg and flour. Again, mix thoroughly with spatula. Place evenly into individual oven-proof dishes and bake in water bath for 1 hour at 375°, or wrap and freeze.

*The Grill at Hacienda del Sol is one of the relatively new kids on Tucson's
fine dining block. It opened August 3, 1997, in the height of that summer's
monsoon season at the then newly renovated Hacienda del Sol Resort.*

The Grill at
Hacienda del Sol

HACIENDA DEL SOL
GUEST RANCH RESORT

The Grill at Hacienda del Sol

5601 N Hacienda del Sol Road
529-3500
Serving Dinner and
Sunday Brunch
$$$$

The Hacienda del Sol Resort is rich in history, starting life as a school for girls in 1929 before it was transformed into a guest ranch in the early 1940s. The sprawling property is studded with native desert vegetation left to flourish among Spanish colonial casitas and classic Mexican adobe architecture. It provided a perfect desert hideaway for movie stars and celebrities like Howard Hughes, Spencer Tracy, Katharine Hepburn, Joseph Cotton, Clark Gable and John Wayne. Urban legend has it that Tracy fell in love with Hepburn at the resort. True or not, there's a room there with his name on it.

The Grill, with talented Chef Jason Jonilonis at the helm, serves up a culinary symphony of American grill classics: regional fish and seafood prepared with Southwest touches; grilled steak dusted with peppercorns; maple and pecan crusted colorado lamb; and a perfectly rare ahi marinated in a Vietnamese chile paste. The menu changes with the seasons, but there's always Pan seared Duck Breast and Pecan Wood Grilled Buffalo Sirloin. Everything is prepared with seasonal ingredients, many of them grown in the Chef Jonilonis' restaurant garden. The resort also grows herbs in decorative pots and incorporates them into the resort landscaping.

"The Grill has a lot of Pacific Rim influences, as well as Southwestern. It's incredibly good and beautifully presented food," said Diane Fausett, the Grill's general manager. "The atmosphere is sumptuous and yet it is very comfortable. It's not a place where you worry about picking up the wrong fork."

Desserts are decadent and memorable. A Hacienda Molten Chocolate Cake that's "cakey" on the outside and oozing with melted chocolate in the middle was a feature of a recent menu. For ultimate indulgence, you could order it topped with ice cream. Equally decadent was a recent Raspberry Passion Fruit Pyramid, featuring a not-too-sweet mousse with a thin cake base surrounded by a raspberry coulis.

The Grill has hosted Primavera Cooks! since 2003 and the apprentices love working with Chef Jonilonis.

The Grill at Hacienda del Sol
September 2003

EXECUTIVE CHEF

Albert Hall

APPRENTICE CHEFS

Georgia Duncan
Robyn Hardy
Peter Schroeder
Nina Trasoff

"Plating and garnishing finish the masterpiece." ~Robyn Hardy

"Astounding to see this many people in such close quarters with hot stoves and knives." ~Nina Trasoff

First Course Croustade of Sonoma Valley Chevre, Roasted Plum Tomatoes and Garden Basil Pesto, House Cured Scottish Salmon, Beluga Caviar, Red Onion and Aquavit Crema, Tellicherry Pepper Crusted Breast of Duck Canapés, Baby Frisée and Wild Lingonberry Relish, Poke of Hawaiian Big Eye Tuna, Caramelized Pineapple and Asian Slaw Won Tons • Castello di Spessa Sauvignon Blanc

Second Course Dinner: Paupiette of Fresh Petrale Sole Filled with Smoked Sablefish Mousse, Braised Baby Spinach and Golden Beets Sauce Vin Blanc, Rouille • Healdsburg Vineyards Chardonnay

Third Course Salad of Wood Roasted Quail, Watercress, Fuji Apples, Spiced Pecans, Point Reyes Farmstead Blue Cheese and White Balsamic-Pear Vinaigrette • Flora Springs Sangiovese

Fourth Course Wood Fired Mixed Grill, Summerfield Farms Baby Lamb Chop, Petit Mignon Tenderloin, Bordeaux Wine Sauce with Hudson Valley Foie Gras and Fresh Truffles, Fresh Vegetables in Miniature, Wild Mushroom Polenta • Codice Tinto Tempranillo

Fifth Course Vanilla Bean Crème Brûlée, Chocolate Molten Cake, Trio of House Made Sorbets

Left to right: Nina Trasoff, Albert Hall, Georgia Duncan, Robyn Hardy, and Peter Schroeder (top left photo)

Tellicherri Pepper Crusted Breast of Duck Canapés with Baby Frisée and Wild Lingonberry

INGREDIENTS

Lingonberry Relish
½ cup red wine vinegar
½ cup apple cider vinegar
1 cup sugar
1 teaspoon orange rind or zest, grated
1 quart fresh frozen lingonberries

Fried Won Tons
12 fried won ton skins
peanut or canola oil for frying

Duck
1, 8–10 ounce boneless
    duck breast
24 Tellicherri peppercorns,
    crushed course
pinch Kosher salt
1 head baby frisée
drizzle olive oil
½ drizzle raspberry vinegar
2 tablespoons lingonberry relish
1 tablespoons chives,
    sliced very thin
balsamic reduction

For Lingonberry Relish Simmer all ingredients for 45 minutes. Relish will gel when cooled. Store refrigerated for up to two weeks. Use it as a condiment or an ingredient in vinaigrettes and marinades.

For Fried Won Tons Fill a small saucepan with oil 3 inches deep, heat over medium until the oil is 350°. Reduce heat to maintain temperature. Cut won tons in half from corner to corner creating a triangle; form skins in the shape of a crane/basket. Float won ton triangle flat on surface of hot oil. Use a 1 inch wooden dowel or whisk handle to submerge the won ton far enough so that the pointed ends bend upwards. Fry until crisp and golden brown, about 30 seconds. Remove from oil and drain on a paper towel lined plate. Reserve for assembly.

For Duck Split duck breast into 2 pieces, removing cartilage from the center. Trim excess fat from the edges and score the skin side of the breasts. Place in refrigerator until they are to be cooked. Season the duck breasts with the Kosher salt and cracked Tellicherri pepper. Heat a skillet over high heat and sauté the duck breasts skin side down in a dry skillet. When the fat begins to render, reduce heat to medium-high and continue cooking for 3-4 minutes or until the skin is crispy. Turn and continue to cook to desired doneness (another 3-4 minutes for medium rare to medium). Remove from skillet and let cool to room temperature. Slice the duck thin on the bias. Reserve at room temperature. Rinse the frisée and pat dry. Chiffonnade ¼ of the frisée and place in small bowl. Season with salt, pepper and a drizzle of olive oil and a half drizzle of raspberry vinegar, or your favorite vinegar. Toss well.

Platting Place the fried won tons on a cookie sheet. Take a small pinch of the seasoned frisée and place in center. Take one slice of duck breast and with both hands, twist the ends in opposite directions for one complete revolution. Bring the two ends together and place duck over the frisée. A small dollop of lingonberry relish is then placed over the duck and is garnished with chopped chives. When all the canapés are finished place on a decorated platter. Before serving, pass several ribbons of aged balsamic reduction over the whole platter.

The Grill at Hacienda del Sol
September 2004

EXECUTIVE CHEF

Jason Jonilonis

APPRENTICE CHEFS

Dave Gallaher
Melinda Kay
Rebecca McReynolds
Sandy Mitchel
Andrew Stewart

"How hot it was! What a treat to be sent to the freezer for something."
~Sandy Mitchel

"We prepared the meal from top to bottom." ~Andrew Stewart

First Course Passed Hors d'oeuvres: Seared Diver Scallops with Oven Dried Green Apple and Tomatillo Honey Compote, Jalapeño Spiced Spinach and Manchego Cheese Pinenut Phyllo Pouches, Rock Shrimp and Pear Brochettes, Tangerine Gaujillo Chile Glaze • Korbel Natural Champagne

Second Course Seared Alaskan Halibut Salad, End of Summer Stone Fruit Compote, Spicy Micro Greens Salad, Herbed Goat Cheese Crostini • Bon Terra Viognier

Third Course Braised Muscovey Duck, Peppered Smoked Duck Bacon, Sun Dried Cherry Toasted Pecan Risotto • Italia Bolo Forte Merlot

Fourth Course Seared Angus Fillet Mignon, Maytag Blue Cheese Duchess Potatoes, Caramelized Shallot Bordelaise • Mariah Zinfandel

Fifth Course Flourless Chocolate DecaDense, Brown Sugar Glazed Figs, Aged Balsamic Hazelnut Ice Cream • Jekel Carbernet

Left to right: Rebecca McReynolds, Melinda Kay, Sandy Mitchel, Andrew Stewart, Dave Gallaher, and Jason Jonilonis

Seared Angus Fillet Mignon with Caramelized Shallot Jus

INGREDIENTS

Veal Stock

3 pounds veal shank bones

1 cup each of onions, carrots,
   celery, roughly chopped

6 garlic cloves

1 ham hock, smoked water

1 tablespoon cracked black peppercorns

6 thyme sprigs

8 parsley sprigs

3 bay leaves

1 pint cherry tomatoes

olive oil

Brown Sauce

1 pound of meat scraps, cleaned

2 tablespoons cracked black peppercorns

½ cup each of onions, carrots,
   celery, roughly chopped

¼ cup tomato paste

3 cups Cabernet or burgundy wine

2 bay leaves

4 sprigs of thyme

1 tablespoons garlic, minced

1 ham hock, smoked

2½ quarts veal stock

olive oil

Caramelized Shallot Jus

½ cup onions, julienned

1 cup shallots, julienned

1 tablespoon garlic, chopped

1 teaspoon cracked black peppercorns

½ bottle Cabernet Sauvignon

1 quart brown sauce

olive oil

thyme sprigs

bay leaves

salt and pepper

For Veal Stock Prepare veal stock one day in advance. Rinse the veal bones under cool running water. Then place the bones in a roasting pan and lightly coat with olive oil. Roast in a 375° oven for about 45-50 minutes until golden brown. Place veal bones in a large stock pot. In the bone roasting pan, drain fat and add onions, celery carrots and garlic. Cook in 375° oven for about 15-20 minutes until lightly caramelized. Add the vegetables to the large stock pot. Cover bones and vegetables with about 1½ gallons of water. Add ham hock, peppercorns, thyme, parsley, and cherry tomatoes. Bring to a boil, then reduce to a very low heat and slow simmer for 12-18 hours. Strain and set aside. Skim fat off the top of the stock.

For Brown Sauce In a large saucepot, sear the meat scraps with the cracked peppercorns. Add onions, carrots and celery in 2 tablespoons of olive oil and sauté for approximately 6-10 minutes. Add tomato paste and stir to prevent sticking to the bottom of the pan. Deglaze with the red wine. Reduce red wine until almost dry. Add bay leaves, thyme sprigs, garlic and ham hock. Add the veal stock and reduce by half.

For Caramelized Shallot Jus In a large sauce pot, caramelize the onions and shallots in olive oil over medium low heat, until light caramel in color. Add garlic, peppercorns and deglaze with Cabernet. Reduce until almost dry, then add 1 quart of brown sauce. Add thyme sprigs and bay leaves. Simmer for about 2 hours to desired consistency, while periodically skimming the foam off the top. Season to taste with salt and pepper, then strain.

The Grill at Hacienda del Sol
September 2005

EXECUTIVE CHEF

Craig Dibbern

APPRENTICE CHEFS

Fran Emrick
Hank Schweighardt
Patrick Straney
Eddie Gilliam

*" Such a large number of people,
each working on their specialty,
orchestrated by Maestro Chef Craig."
~Patrick Straney*

*"It was interesting to see the difference
between what's available to restaurants from their suppliers and what
we can find in our grocery stores."
~Eddie Gilliam*

First Course Passed Hors d'oeuvres: Seared Sea Diver Scallops with Oven Roasted Pineapple Mango Salsa, Chorizo Jalapeño Spiced Spinach and Manchego Cheese Stuffed Mushrooms, Southwestern Bruschetta • J.F. Lurton Pinot Gris

Second Course Butterleaf, Mesclun, White Anchovies and Heirloom Tomatoes with Garden Basil White Balsamic Vinaigrette, Olive Tapenade Crostini • J.F. Lurton Pinot Gris

Third Course Braised Duck Confit Spring Roll, Peppered Smoked Duck Bacon, Butter Braised Maui Onions, Duck Demi • Elsa Malbec

Fourth Course Roasted Tenderloin of Angus Beef, Truffle Risotto, Caramelized Shallot Sage Bordelaise and Baby Vegetables • Turner Road Cabernet Sauvignon

Fifth Course Caramel Chocolate Bomb, Hazelnut Cookie, Raspberry Compote, Coffee

Left to right: Eddie Gilliam, Fran Emrick, Craig Dibbern, Hank Schweighardt, and Patrick Straney

Seared Diver Scallops with Oven Roasted Pineapple and Mango Salsa

INGREDIENTS

Scallops with Pineapple and Mango Salsa
2 large diver scallops
1 each small red onion
½ cup pineapple, diced small
¼ cup mango, diced small
pinch of cilantro
salt and pepper to taste

Peel foot off scallops, rinse and set aside. Place whole red onion in oven safe bowl whole and cover lightly with olive oil. Wrap bowl with aluminum foil and place in a 350° oven until soft. Spread pineapple on silpat mat in one even layer. Sprinkle with salt and pepper and place in a 200° oven for 1 hour. Finely dice red onion and toss with pineapple and mango. Add cilantro salt and pepper to taste. Season both sides of scallops and sear on each side until golden brown, about 3 minutes per side. Place on serving tray and top each scallop with a little of the Pineapple Mango Salsa. Serve hot.

Truffle Risotto

INGREDIENTS

Risotto
3 tablespoons olive oil
1 cup arborio rice
3 cups chicken stock
2 cups heavy cream
1 tablespoon truffle peelings, chopped
salt and pepper to taste

Heat oil in 2 quart skillet, add rice and stir until coated with oil. Add chicken stock 1 cup at a time stirring frequently until, cook until liquid is almost completely absorbed before adding more. Add heavy cream when all out of chicken stock; mix well until almost dry. Mix in truffle peelings, salt and pepper to taste.

The menu at Janos Wilder's restaurant changes with the seasons. He estimates that he has featured 10,000 meals on the menu since opening in 1983 at his original location in an adobe house on the grounds of the Tucson Museum of Art. Within a year of opening, Janos was garnering critical acclaim both locally and nationally. The New York Times reviewed it favorably and Playboy magazine named it one of the nation's top eateries. Janos became such a hot spot that it outgrew its downtown adobe and moved to La Paloma for more elbowroom. That same year, 1998, Wilder opened a less-expensive adjoining sister restaurant, called J BAR.

Janos

Janos

3770 E Sunrise Drive
615-6100
Serving Dinner
Closed Monday
$$$$

For a truly lavish night of dining, many Tucsonans choose Janos at Westin La Paloma Resort. It's a special-night-out spot that delivers the ultimate fantasy dining experience: wait staff that is attentive but not intrusive in an ambiance that is elegant and romantic, without being stifling.

However, it is the French-inspired Southwest cuisine that steals your attention. Appetizers like a roasted lobster tail with smoked mushroom flan and butternut squash blini, or a rich lobster and wild mushroom bisque are perfect beginnings for Pecan Crusted Scottish Salmon with blue posole broth and sizzling chile butter; Ten Hour Beef Short Ribs served with horseradish spiked mashed potatoes, orange mojo and candied kumquats; Bacon and Gorgonzola Stuffed Chicken with a peppered peach and basil salad and olive oil and chive crushed Yukon Gold potatoes. End the evening on a sweet note as you linger over the house special dark chocolate jalapeño ice cream sundae while sipping a lovely glass of Chambers Tokay from Australia.

In 2000, Wilder added a very bright feather to his glowing culinary cap when the prestigious James Beard Foundation named him top chef in the Southwest. He's the only chef in Tucson to boast the Beard medal, which honors chefs for innovation and excellence.

Wilder's involvement with Primavera predates Tucson Original's Primavera Cooks! project. The chef and his family have, for the past decade, prepared a monthly meal for Primavera program residents. "I like Primavera's grassroots approach," Wilder said. "They serve meals, seven days a week and they get a different organization in there to prepare each meal. That's more than 100 local organizations a month."

Janos particularly enjoys the Primavera Cooks! Events. These allow him to involve his staff, as they work directly with the apprentice chefs. "It's a great thing for an apprentice chef," he said. "They get a glimpse at the professional kitchen, and it's a great thing for our chefs, as well, to show off what they know."

Janos
May 2004

EXECUTIVE CHEF

Janos Wilder

APPRENTICE CHEFS

Larry Kelsey
Mike Nicholas
Ron Newman

"Never a dull moment and fortunately all the staff were very accommodating." ~Larry Kelsey

"Being an amateur chef, I jumped at the opportunity to work in one of Tucson's finest restaurants but I guess the main reason I participated was to support a great cause- Primavera."
~Mike Nicholas

First Course Fava Beans, Asparagus and Heirloom Tomatoes on Creamy Mascarpone Polenta with Roasted Corn Coulis, Tomato Water, Basil and Thyme • Casa Lapostolle Sauvignon Blanc

Second Course Seared Day Boat Sea Scallop on Wild Rice Cake with Chipotle Muscat Sauce with Salmon Caviar, Candied Orange Zest and Micro Greens • Casa Lapostolle 'Cuvee Alexandre' Chardonnay

Third Course Pan-Seared Halibut with Braised Cippolini Onions, Artichokes and Baby Corn on Minted Pea Coulis with Ratatouille Vinaigrette • Casa Lapostolle 'Cuvee Alexandre' Merlot

Fourth Course Grilled New York Strip on Robuchon's Potato Gratin with Truffle Mushrooms, Whittled Asparagus and Red Wine Reduction • Casa Lapostolle 'Cuvee Alexandre' Cabernet Sauvignon

Fifth Course Strawberry, Grand Marnier Phyllo Napoleons • Grand Marnier

Left to right: Mike Nicholas, Larry Kelsey, and Ron Newman

Napoleon of Strawberries and Grand Marnier Cream

INGREDIENTS

Grand Marnier Cream

1 cup whipping cream
sugar to sweeten
3 tablespoons Grand Marnier
6 crisp phyllo squares
12 strawberries, cut in half
    lengthwise and hulled
2 ounces strawberry coulis
mint

Crispy Phyllo Layers

5 sheets phyllo
¼ pound butter
1 cup granulated sugar

For Cream Whip the cream to soft peaks adding the sugar to taste and the Grand Marnier right at the end. Layer the phyllo with the strawberries and whipped cream 3 layers high. Garnish plate with the strawberry coulis and mint.

For Phyllo Lay 1 sheet of phyllo flat on a sheet pan. Brush with butter then sprinkle with sugar. Lay another sheet of phyllo on top and repeat using all five sheets. Cut the sheets into 6 equal size squares or other appropriate size. Place a second sheet pan on top of the phyllo to hold them in place. Bake at 350° for about 15 minutes or until golden.

Creamy Polenta with Mascarpone

INGREDIENTS

Polenta with Mascarpone

2 cups whole milk
½ cup medium grain
    yellow cornmeal
3 tablespoons mascarpone
Kosher salt
freshly ground pepper
additional warm milk
    as needed to thin

In a stainless steel pan bring milk to a boil. To avoid lumps, slowly sprinkle the cornmeal into the milk whisking constantly until the cornmeal is completely absorbed and fairly thick. Turn heat to very low and stir constantly until well thickened and raw taste is gone, about 20 minutes. Stir in cheese, add salt and pepper to taste. Reheat by slowly warming with hot milk until quite creamy.

Janos
May 2005

EXECUTIVE CHEF

Janos Wilder

APPRENTICE CHEFS

Stephen Golden
Jeff Grubic
Ron Newman
Susan Tarrence

"Of all the knowledge I acquired during my time at Janos, the secrets of working with pig caul and the nuances of the assembly of baklava stand out." ~Jeff Grubic

"What a great way to make money for a wonderful organization."
~Susan Tarrence and Stephen Golden"

First Course Terrine of Smoked Salmon, Shrimp and Scallops, Savory Chive Cheese Cake, Whipped Cream, Cider and Apple Vinaigrette and Tangle of Basil Shoots • Dynamite Sauvignon Blanc

Second Course Chicken Breast and Mushrooms in Puff Pastry with Toasted Orzo, Summer Squash, Wilted Spinach and Whole Grain Mustard Sauce • Echelon Chardonnay

Third Course Orange-Mustard BBQ Pork Tenderloin with Vinegary Cucumber-Jicama Slaw Served On Cornbread Crouton with Gherkins, Grilled Corn and Buttermilk Sauce • Echelon Pinot Noir

Fourth Course Ten Hour Braised Beef Short Rib, Basil Mojo and Candied Kumquats, Horseradish Mashed Potatoes, Mint Glazed Carrots and Sauce from the Braising Liquid • Sageland Cabernet Sauvignon

Fifth Course Dessert Baklava with White Peach Ice Cream, Orange Scented Honey Syrup • Beaulieu Vineyards Orange Muscat

Left to right: Stephen Golden, Susan Tarrence, Jeff Grubic, and Ron Newman

Ten Hour Braised Beef Short Ribs with Horseradish Mashed Potatoes and Glazed Minted Carrots

INGREDIENTS

Ribs

6 large short ribs with bone,
    about 1 pound each
1 cup carrots, chopped
1 cup celery, chopped
1 cup yellow onions, chopped
2 cups red wine
1 quart veal or beef stock (*recipe
    in Hacienda del Sol section)
4 stems fresh thyme
salt and freshly cracked black pepper
clarified butter, grapeseed oil, or canola
    oil for searing the short ribs.

Mashed Potatoes

3 large russet potatoes, peeled and
    cut into large, evenly sized pieces
2 tablespoons salt for the water
⅓ pound butter
½ cup heavy cream or half and half
3 tablespoons prepared horseradish
salt and pepper to taste

Carrots

18 baby carrots, peeled
water to cover
2 teaspoons sugar
2 tablespoons unsalted butter
pinch salt
4 sprigs fresh mint

For Ribs Liberally salt and pepper the short ribs. Heat heavy pan with a thin layer of oil. Sear all sides of the short ribs and remove from pan. Add the vegetables and cook for 6-8 minutes to brown them slightly. Remove from pan and place on the bottom of braising dish. Add the red wine to deglaze the pan. Place the browned short ribs on the vegetables. Pour the wine and veal stock over the meat to cover. Add the thyme. Cover and cook in 250° oven 8-10 hours. Remove the short ribs from the liquid and let them cool. Strain the liquid and reserve for sauce and for storing the short ribs. Remove the bone from the short ribs and trim off excess fat. Store the ribs in the sauce and heat gently in the sauce pouring excess sauce over the ribs.

For Potatoes In a large pot bring potatoes, salt and a large volume of cold water to a boil. Reduce to simmer for about 10 minutes until the potatoes are quite tender. Drain off the water. In the meantime, in a saucepan, heat the butter and cream to a simmer and reduce heat. Run the potatoes through a potato ricer. In a large bowl, thoroughly mix together potatoes, cream sauce and horseradish. Season with salt and pepper to taste.

For Carrots In large pan place carrots with enough room that they may move freely, then cover with cold water, sugar, butter, salt and mint. Bring to a boil and then reduce to a simmer. Simmer about 10-15 minutes until the vegetables are the desired softness. The liquid should be just about evaporated at this time. If needed, add extra water, or pour off excess water. Remove the mint and roll the carrots to glaze well.

Jonathan's Tucson Cork started life in 1966 as part of the popular
Arizona steak and seafood chain Cork and Cleaver. In 1994, Jonathan
and Colette Landeen took it over, changed the name and set the course
for the eatery's tasty future.

Jonathan describes his restaurant as "elegant dining in a casual atmosphere."
You'll often see him with his handlebar mustache and floral-printed
parachute pants in the dining room conversing with diners about what they
thought of their meals.

Jonathan's
Tucson Cork

Jonathan's Tucson Cork

6320 E Tanque Verde Road
296-1631
Serving Dinner
$$$

The Landeens carefully maintained some of the restaurant's beloved menu items while recrafting the offerings to include Landeen's original creations, many reflecting his New Orleans training. Landeen trained under the guidance of celebrated chef Paul Prudhomme. Fans of the Cork and Cleaver days can skip down the menu to "Cork Traditions" and order up a number of steaks, from New York to prime rib. Guests can also request the ever-popular "baseball," an 11 or 12-ounce top sirloin marinated in teriyaki and grilled. It was originally called the Cork's Pride, but because of its shape and, possibly as homage to the UA softball, the name was changed.

The chef's creativity sparkles throughout the menu. You might start with the blackened chicken and calamari appetizers or the exquisite escargot swimming in rich garlic butter. Ahi steak, cooked a perfect medium rare, is seared with a bold ginger rub and served with sake ginger. Sweet gulf shrimp are brushed with a red chili sauce before they are grilled to the perfect tenderness and served with a delightful pistachio cilantro pesto.

Jonathan's offers several wild game dishes, including a beefy charbroiled ostrich steak or a bison fillet wrapped with jalapeño bacon. Landeen also added liver and onions, roast duck and chicken.

Award-winning pastry chef Peggy Forrest chimes in with decadent desserts: Almond Roche Cake, crème brûlée, Mud Pie, a buttery lemon pound cake with raspberry purée and a New Orleans-style bread pudding with a rich butter sauce.

Landeen, the current president of Tucson Originals, has supported Primavera Cooks! since it started in 2002. "It's fun and it's a good cause. It's fun for the staff, and it's not a difficult thing to do because you don't have to leave your kitchen." "We've had a lot of success with it," he said. "One year we had a group of apprentice chefs who wanted to do things their way and make it into a private party so they bought the event out. That kind of made it interesting."

Jonathan's Tucson Cork
September 2002

EXECUTIVE CHEF

Jonathan Landeen

APPRENTICE CHEFS

Peter Schroeder
Georgia Duncan
Steve Pageau

"This restaurant operates with only one 38" range!" ~Georgia Duncan

"I now understand the saying, 'if you can't stand the heat, stay out of the kitchen.' " ~Steve Pageau

First Course Hors d'oeuvres • McPhearson Shiraz or Fontana Candida Pinot Grigio

Second Course Gazpacho with Green Onion, Cilantro, and Cream

Third Course Lime Broiled Cabrilla with Red Chili Cream and Roasted Red Bell Pepper Garnish • Fetzer Barrel Select Chardonnay

Fourth Course Watermelon Granitée

Fifth Course Mixed Grill of Pistachio Crusted Lamb Chop, Sautéed Venison Medallions, and Charbroiled Ostrich with Yukon Gold Potatoes and Baby Vegetables • Fetzer "Barrel Select" Cabernet Sauvignon

Sixth Course Crème Brûlée with Fresh Fruit • Lindemans Botrytised Semillon

Left to right: Steve Pageau, Georgia Duncan, Jonathan Landeen, and Peter Schroeder

Watermelon Granitée

INGREDIENTS

Watermelon Granitée
3 cups of watermelon juice
1 cup sugar
4 pounds of watermelon,
   seedless in chunks
2 tablespoons of fresh lemon juice
½ cup pomegranate concentrate

In a small saucepan reduce watermelon juice to ⅓, add sugar and stir until dissolved. Let cool. In a food processor purée watermelon and add sugar mixture, lemon juice, and pomegranate concentrate. Pour into a baking dish and place in freezer. Stir every 30 minutes until completely frozen—about 3 hours. Spoon into dishes and serve frozen.

Lime Broiled Cabrilla with Roasted Red Chili Sauce

INGREDIENTS

Broiled Cabrilla
6, 7-ounce fillets of cabrilla
2 limes
½ cup white wine
dry mild red chili flakes

Red Chili Sauce
2 cups white wine
1 cup shrimp stock
4 ounces New Mexico red
   chili purée, uncooked
flour
1 cup whipping cream
water

For Broiled Cabrilla Place fish on baking dish, squeeze on juice from limes and splash with wine. Lightly sprinkle with chili flakes. Broil for approximately 8 minutes until done and serve with red chili cream sauce.

For Red Chili Sauce In sauce pan, reduce white wine by half. Add shrimp stock and chili purée and bring to boil. Tighten with flour and water and stir in cream.

Jonathan's Tucson Cork
September 2003

EXECUTIVE CHEF

Jonathan Landeen

APPRENTICE CHEFS

Kathy Arrotta
Joe Heller
Carol and Neil West

"Chef says — taste something three times and clear the palate in between." ~Joe Heller

"Organization came out of seeming chaos. We love being a part of this great event." ~Carol and Neil West

First Course Passed Hors d'oeuvres, Martinis or Champagne, Gravlax with Artic Char presented with Tomato Concasse and Crepe Pinwheels • Acacia Pinot Noir

Second Course Shrimp One One One, Lemon Grapefruit, Red Chili Cilantro and Bombay • Cloudy Bay Sauvignon Blanc

Third Course Cream of Spinach and Watercress Soup • Murphy Goode Island Block Chardonnay

Fourth Course Duck Galantine with Pistachio Nuts, Roasted Antelope Sirloin with Apple Glaze, Cajun Pecans and Axis Venison Chop with a Green Peppercorn Glaze, Wild Mushroom, Red Himalayan Rice, Butternut Squash and Haricot Vert • Joseph Phelps "Le Mistral" Syrah Blend

Fifth Course Chocolate Truffles with a Blueberry Ginger Granita • Selected Port

Left to right: Carol and Neil West, Joe Heller, Jonathan Landeen, and Kathy Arrotta

Duck Galantine

INGREDIENTS

Duck

3 tablespoons seasoned salt

5 eggs

6 tablespoons brandy

2 pounds pork fat

½ pound veal, finely ground

1 pound duck, finely ground

8 ounces pistachio nuts

stock

For Duck Push seasoned salt (recipe below), eggs and brandy though a sieve then blend into meats and nuts with a wooden spoon until mixture is smooth. Wrap mixture in duck skin or Saran Wrap and then wrap in cheesecloth. Tie ends like a sausage. Poach in stock for approximately 45 minutes. When pierced with fork, juice should run clear.

Seasoned Salt

INGREDIENTS

Salt

¼ teaspoon bay leaf, powdered

¼ teaspoon thyme, powdered

¼ teaspoon cloves, powdered

¼ teaspoon cinnamon, powdered

¼ teaspoon nutmeg, powdered

¼ teaspoon ginger, powdered

¼ teaspoon mace, powdered

¼ teaspoon coriander, powdered

¾ teaspoon black and white pepper,
    mixed together

3 teaspoons salt

pinch cayenne

Mix all ingredients together. Reserve as a condiment for table service or recipes.

Jonathan's Tucson Cork
September 2004

EXECUTIVE CHEF

Jonathan Landeen

APPRENTICE CHEFS

Susan Aguirre
Kathy Arrotta
Eli Stinger

"Working with a professional chef was a real kick. They are like a walking cookbook." ~Kathy Arrotta

"Primavera is a great organization and I am glad to do something to help." ~Susan Aguirre

First Course Rock Shrimp and Cucumber Salad with a Raspberry Vinaigrette • Chalk Hill Chardonnay

Second Course Hot Italian Sausage and Black Mussels over Fresh Fettuccini with Steak Tomatoes Concasse • Russian Hill River Pinot Noir

Intermezzo Apples, Apples, Apples

Third Course Lamb Sausage and Creole Mustard Cream • Alexander Valley Vineyard Merlot

Fourth Course Pig on the Spit with Beets, Napa Cabbage and Fingerling Potatoes • Alden Vineyard Cabernet Sauvignon

Fifth Course German Chocolate Cake

Left to right: Laurent Poissonnet, Eli Stinger, Jonathan Landeen, Kathy Arrotta, and Susan Aguirre

Rock Shrimp, Cucumber and Raspberry Vinaigrette Salad

INGREDIENTS

Salad

1 pound cooked rock shrimp, chilled

½ teaspoon Dijon mustard

juice of half a lemon

¼ cup raspberry vinegar

1 cup of extra virgin olive oil

pinch salt

pinch pepper

1 medium red bell pepper, medium diced

1 red onion, medium diced

2 medium cucumbers, peeled, seeded
   and diced large

red salad Savoy leaves

sugar, if desired

In a medium glass bowl, mix mustard, lemon juice and vinegar. Blend in olive oil to smooth consistency; continue stirring; add salt, pepper, bell pepper and onion. Toss in cucumber and allow to rest for one hour in the refrigerator. Check the flavor and add additional salt and pepper and a little bit of sugar if you would like. Toss in rock shrimp. Place one or two salad Savoy leaves in a large martini glass; fill with shrimp mixture and serve.

Tomato Concasse with Italian Sausage and Black Mussels

INGREDIENTS

Concasse

2 red beefsteak tomatoes, peeled
   seeded and coarsely chopped

2 yellow beefsteak tomatoes, peeled
   seeded and coarsely chopped

¼ cup parsley, chopped

2 tablespoon cilantro, chopped

¼ cup extra virgin olive oil

2 cloves garlic, minced

1 medium shallot, minced

salt and black pepper, to taste

Sausage and Mussels

2 pounds black mussels

8, ¼-pound hot Italian sausage links

For Concasse In medium bowl, mix together tomatoes and remaining ingredients.

For Sausage and Mussels Steam mussels and hold warm. Reserve ¼ cup of the juice. In large pan, sauté sausage, remove from pan and slice. Return to pan with black mussels and mussel juice. Toss and serve over pasta and top with Tomato Concasse.

Jonathan's Tucson Cork
September 2005

EXECUTIVE CHEF

Jonathan Landeen

APPRENTICE CHEFS

Rick Arreola
Larry Kelsey
Ron Newman

Appetizers Assorted • Bogle Sauvignon Blanc

First Course Catfish with a Pecan Meuniere • Bogle Chardonnay

Second Course Salad • Bogle Zinfandel

Third Course Crawfish Etouffee • Bogle Phantom

Intermetzo Pomegranate Sorbet

Fourth Course Filet with a Debris Sauce served with Dirty Rice
and Fresh Vegetable • Bogle Petite Syrah

Fifth Course Grand Marnier Parfait with a Tuile

*"Couldn't believe the intensity level in
the kitchen." ~Rick Arreola*

*"I saw how a good chef could turn
our small mistakes into attractive,
delicious successes." ~Ron Newman*

Left to right: Larry Kelsey, Ron Newman, Rick Arreola, and Jonathan Landeen

Remoulade Sauce

INGREDIENTS

Sauce

2 eggs

juice from 1 lemon

1 cup yellow mustard

1 cup creole mustard

¼ cup white vinegar

1 cup vegetable oil

¾ celery, chopped

½ cup green onions, chopped

½ cup parsley, chopped

¼ cup horseradish

1 bay leaf

1 cup catsup

¼ cup Worcestershire sauce

½ tablespoons tabasco

dash of cayenne

1 tablespoon fresh garlic, minced

Beat eggs, lemon juice, mustards, and vinegar together. Add oil slowly. Whip in rest of ingredients and let still overnight. This is a great chilled dip to be served with cooked shrimp or crab.

Almond Tuile Cookies

INGREDIENTS

Cookies

3 ounces unsalted butter

1½ cup light corn syrup

½ cup brown sugar

pinch of Kosher salt

½ cup of sliced almonds,
   roughly chopped

½ cup all purpose flour

Preheat oven to 350°. In a small saucepan over medium heat, melt butter and corn syrup together. Add brown sugar and salt, stir until dissolved. Remove from heat. Stir almonds and flour into butter mixture until completely incorporated. Line a baking sheet with a silpat or sheet of parchment paper and spoon two teaspoons of batter. Because batter spreads thin when it bakes, spoon only five rounds of batter at a time. Bake in oven until golden brown, about 10 minutes. Remove from oven and let tuile rest on the pan at room temperature until cool enough to handle, about one minute. While the cookie is still warm and pliable, shape into rolls, over the back of a small bowl or over a rolling pin. If the tuile cools before being shaped, place in oven for about 30 seconds, remove and shape immediately. Store tuiles in an airtight container.

Four months after it opened a dozen years ago, Kingfisher's late-night hours attracted nary a soul. Tucson wasn't quite sophisticated enough to enjoy the regional American and seafood eatery's late-night menu. But Kingfisher owners James Murphy, Jeff Azersky and Tim Ivankovich persevered. Today, Kingfisher hops from lunch until late at night when regulars fill the cozy midtown restaurant with bubbly chatter in between bites of savory grilled meats and succulent, inventive seafood. Live music adds to the enjoyment several nights a week.

Kingfisher Bar & Grill

KINGFISHER
An American Grill

Kingfisher Bar & Grill

2564 E Grant Road
323-7739
Serving Lunch, Dinner,
Late Night
$$$-$$$$

Jim Murphy, who shares executive chef duties with Jeff Azersky, says the restaurant's strength lies in its straightforward, consistent approach. "Nothing too fancy, but very straightforward, full-flavored, simply stated," he explains.

The restaurant changes its menu from top to bottom regularly, inviting new dishes that maintain its goal of American regional cuisine and seafood. Regularly you will find oysters served with grilled shrimp and scallop ceviche, clam chowder that reminds you of how they make it in New England; a Grilled Yellowfin Tuna dressed in a rich peppered black bean sauce with a roasted corn salsa and Barbequed Pork Ribs. Desserts, created by pastry chef Marianne Banes, are simple but decadent: Chocolate Mocha Ice Cream Torte served with a rich chocolate sauce, Lime Cheesecake with a toasted almond coconut crust, and the most amazingly refreshing Lemon Tiramisu that caused the *Arizona Daily Star* to gush, "Rarely do you find a restaurant that exceeds your expectations in a way that makes you want to hug your server."

Kingfisher also has made a name for itself with its annual summer Road Trips that present regional flavors that span the country. This past summer, diners visited the Midwest and sipped Wisconsin Cheddar and Wheat Beer Soup followed by Indiana Duckling cooked two ways with peach barbecue sauce. The culinary journey made stops in the Northwest, East, Great Plains and California and Hawaii.

It has taken the owners of Kingfisher a dozen years to decide to expand on their popular restaurant. In early 2005, the trio opened Bluefin on the city's Northwest side. Eighty-five percent of its menu is devoted to seafood and shellfish.

Kingfisher was one of the original founding hosts of the Primavera Cooks! Apprentice Event and they have continued each year, some times hosting as may as five apprentices. "Murph" does the teaching and as one of the apprentices said "He is a good teacher."

Kingfisher Bar & Grill
September 2002

EXECUTIVE CHEFS

Jeff Azersky
Jim Murphy

APPRENTICE CHEFS

Chris Tanz
Jean Paul Bierny
Bill Bode
Carol and Neil West

"Fifty pounds of potatoes are heavy."
~Bill Bode

"This was an eight-ring circus
creating delicious food. We want
to re-enlist."
~Chris Tanz and Jean Paul Bierny

Appetizers House Smoked Ruby Trout on Potato Rosti, Red Onion Confit, Creme Fraiche, Seared Ahi Tuna-Wasabi, Pickled Ginger • Moet Chandon Brut

First Course Chilled Melon Soup, Chiffonade of Spearmint with Sparkling Ported Melon • Mirrassou Chardonnay

Second Course Marinated Roasted And Carved Tenderloin of Sterling Silver Beef Sautéed Oyster Mushrooms "Calvados", Glace Diviande, Lyonnaise Potatoes • Frog's Leap Zinfandel

Third Course Fresh Meyer Lemon Sorbet

Fourth Course Seared Alaskan Halibut With Stone Fruit Glaze, Tossed Mesclun Green Salad, Balsamic Lemon Dressing • Twomey Merlot

Fifth Course A Medley of Fresh Fruit And Cheese, Chocolate Truffle, Frangipane Filo Tart • Dows 10 Year Tawny Port

Left to right: Neil West, Carol West, Jim Murphy, Bill Bode, Marianne Banes, Chris Tanz, and Jean Paul Bierny

House Smoked Ruby Trout

INGREDIENTS

Ruby Trout

4, 8-ounce ruby trout, split,
    belly flap and head removed,
    split down the back, dorsal
    bones removed
1 cup salt
½ teaspoon ground cumin
½ teaspoon black pepper
4 bay leaves
2 cups brown sugar

Using a coffee grinder, grind pepper and bay into powder, then mix into sugar, salt and cumin. Apply "cure" liberally to both sides of fillets and pat down to cover. Chill for 3 hours. Remove and rinse gently, pat dry and chill one additional hour. Then, hot smoke at 200° or more for 18-20 minutes until fish has reached temp of 165° internally.

Melon Soup

INGREDIENTS

Soup

1 fresh lime, cut in half
3 cups sparkling wine
1 cup apple juice
3 cups crenshaw, cut
3 cups cantaloupe, cut
2 cups honeydew melon,
    prepared in small balls
6 large mint leaves, rolled
    into tubes and cut

In large saucepot, place lime, wine and apple juice in sauce pot. Heat to 170°, then remove and chill. Process crenshaw and cantaloupe in a food processor. Press through sieve, reserve any pulp and chill liquid. In a clean chilled bowl, pour melon liquid and then strain wine mixture, taking care to express all juice from lime. Chill. In chilled bowls place equal amounts of chilled honeydew melon balls and gently pour purée over top. Sprinkle chiffonade mint over top, serve with chilled spoons.

Kingfisher Bar & Grill
September 2003

EXECUTIVE CHEFS

Jeff Azersky
Jim Murphy

APPRENTICE CHEFS

Nancy Bissell
Eddie Gilliam
Starr Sanders
Andy Silverman

*"Smoking trout is 'relatively'
easy and Primavera is the best
organization in town."
~Andy Silverman and Starr Sanders*

*"This whole thing is a real art."
~Nancy Bissell*

First Course Smoked Trout Canape with Herbed Goat Cheese, King Crab Cocktail, en croute, Kalamata Olive Roasted Pepper Bruschetta with Fresh Mozzarella • Easton Natoma Semillion Viognier Chardonnay Blend

Second Course Jumbo Gulf Oyster with Fresh Chanterelle and Cascabel Chili Pan • Foris Pinot Noir

Third Course Composite Salad, Hearts of Romaine, Grape Tomatoes, Roasted Beets, Julienne Carrot, Edamame Sprouts, Roasted Tomato Vinaigrette, Avocado, Shrimp Toast Crouton • Smith Madrone Johannisberg Riesling

Fourth Course Medley of Stuffed Hawaiian Onaga with Dipping Sauce and Roasted Porcini Crusted Tenderloin of Beef with Glace di Viandie Meritage • Waterbrook Melange — Cabernet Merlot Petite Verdot

Fifth Course Fresh Berries Semifreddo, Almond Cookies, Bittersweet Chocolate Sauce • Montevina Zinfandel Port

Left to right: Jim Murphy, Eddie Gilliam, Andy Silverman, Starr Sanders, Nancy Bissell, and Jeff Azersky

Cascabel Chile, Gulf Oyster, and Fresh Chanterelle Pan Roast

INGREDIENTS

Gulf Oyster and Pan Roast

6 Cascabel chilies (soaked in
   1 cup warm water)
2 ounces sweet cream butter
½ cup white onion, minced
1 teaspoon white pepper
1 pinch celery salt
1 teaspoon paprika
2 teaspoons Worcestershire sauce
16 freshly shucked Gulf oysters
   (reserve liquor)
2 teaspoons chile sauce
1 cup heavy cream
½ cup bread crumbs (not stale)
2 cups large diced mushrooms
1 bay leaf
salt and pepper to taste

When chilies are soft, purée in blender until smooth, then strain, reserve liquid, discard the rest. In a large pan melt butter, add onion, pepper, celery salt, paprika, Worcestershire sauce; cook until onions are translucent. Add oysters, liquor, and chile purée, poach gently until oysters start to curl, add cream, heat to simmer, add bread crumbs and remove from heat. In separate pan, sauté the mushrooms over high heat, until hot, add to bottom of bowl, and cover with the soup. Garnish with fresh parsley and serve.

Kingfisher Bar & Grill
September 2004

EXECUTIVE CHEFS

Jeff Azersky
Jim Murphy

APPRENTICE CHEFS

Robyn Hardy
Eddie Gilliam
Gary Albert
Wendy and Allen Gilden

*"Looking forward to next year, it's
a great way to support Primavera."
~Eddie Gilliam*

*"Murph is a great teacher."
~Gary Albert*

First Course Sea of Cortez Cabrilla "Ceviche" Onion, Garlic, Red and Green Peppers, Cilantro Jalapeño, Jicama • Robert Pepi Pinot Grigio

Second Course Roasted Butternut Chowder Squash, Fingerling Potatoes, Fennel, Apple, Sweet Cream, Cascabel Caramel, Shaved Nutmeg • Eberle Chardonnay

Third Course Composite Salad – Asian Micro Mesclun Greens, Ginger Vinaigrette, Bluefin Sashimi Sesame Crouton, Smoked Ruby Trout Crouton, Warm Spicy Avocado Shrimp Crouton • Beckmen "Cuvee LeBec" Rhone Blend

Intermezzo Limoncello Sorbet • Sofia Blanc de Blanc

Fourth Course Beer Tenderloin "Primavera" Sautéed Spinach with Sliced Heirloom Tomatoes, in Puff Pastry with a Wild Mushroom Sauce Vegetable Parisienne • Delectus Meritage "Argentum"

Fifth Course Pecan Crusted Goat Cheese and Mascarpone Tart, Warm Berry Flambé • St. Armant L.B.V Port Lagniappe

Left to right: Gary Albert, Robyn Hardy, Eddie Gilliam, Jim Murphy, Wendy and Allen Gilden

Pecan Crusted Goat Cheese and Mascarpone Tarts

INGREDIENTS

Tarts
20 ounces goat cheese
1½ cup sugar
1 tablespoon lemon juice
1 tablespoon vanilla
1 tablespoon lemon zest
12 eggs, separated
7 tablespoons flour
1 pound mascarpone

Pecan Crust
6 cups flour
1 cup sugar
2 cups cold butter, cut into small pieces
4 eggs
1 tablespoon vanilla
1 teaspoon salt
4 cups finely ground pecans

Combine flour, sugar and butter until crumbly. Add eggs, vanilla and salt and mix until incorporated. Stir in nuts and chill. In mixing bowl, beat goat cheese, sugar, lemon juice, vanilla and zest until smooth. Add yolks two at a time and mix in flour. Then beat to incorporate. Add mascarpone. Do not over mix. In separate bowl beat egg whites. Fold in beaten whites to cheese mixture. Pour incorporated mixture into prepared shells. Bake au bain marie 300° for 20 to 25 minutes.

Limoncello Sorbet

INGREDIENTS

Limoncello Sorbet
4½ cups sugar
6 cups water
2 cups lemon juice
1 cup limoncello
6 lemons zested

In medium pot make a syrup with sugar and water. Bring to a boil, remove, add lemon juice and limoncello. Add zest. Cool and freeze in ice cream maker.

Kingfisher Bar & Grill
September 2005

EXECUTIVE CHEFS

Jeff Azersky
Jim Murphy

APPRENTICE CHEFS

Gary Albert
Shannon McBride-Olson
Mark Rubin
Ann Stevens

"I like getting to taste the ingredients and then seeing how they all work together." ~Ann Stevens

"Primavera is a good organization and I had a lot of fun supporting it." ~Mark Rubin

Appetizers Course Smoked Tilapia, Red Onion Jam, Sourdough Melba, Grilled Cornmeal Crust Wild Mushroom Pizza with Wine Cured Aged Goat Cheese, Baked Stuffed Clams "Storyville"

First Course Creole Barbecue Shrimp, Texmati Pecan Rice Pilaf, Blackened Voodoo Lager, Worcestershire sauce, garlic, butter, parsley • Corazon Gewürztraminer

Second Course Chilled Heirloom Tomato Soup • Palette De Blanc Pretty Smith Sauvignon Blanc Chardonnay Muscat Blend

Third Course Irish Salmon Confit Salad with Braised Fennel, Belgian Red Endive, Arugula Frisee • Macrostie Pinot Noir

Fourth Course Cedar Planked Sturgeon, Grilled Apple Buerre Blanc, Root Vegetable Gratin, Fried Leeks • Ventana Vineyards Syrah Grenache Blend "Beaugravier ", Arroyo Seco, 2000.

Fifth Course Chocolate Bag, Frangelico White Chocolate Mousse, Hazelnut Praline, Macerated Berries • Elysium Black Muscat

Left to Right: Mark Rubin, Marianne Banes, Gary Albert, Jim Murphy, Shannon McBride-Olson, and Ann Stevens

White Chocolate Whipped Cream Mousse

INGREDIENTS

White Chocolate

white chocolate (mousse base)

1 quart heavy cream

22 ounces white chocolate, chopped

Mousse

1 pint heavy whipping cream

1 cup white chocolate cream (denouze)

For White Chocolate Heat cream to scald, remove and pour over white chocolate and stir to melt and blend. When chocolate is completely melted, whisk to blend, cool to 40 degrees, overnight is best.

For Mousse Whip cream to soft peak on low speed. Add white chocolate cream in ribbon, beat until it forms a stiff peak, do not overwhip!

Creole Barbeque Shrimp

INGREDIENTS

Barbeque Shrimp

24 shrimp, peeled

1 cup each dried rosemary,
   cracked black pepper and
   seafood seasoning

1 tablespoon garlic, chopped

2 ounces Worcestershire sauce

12 ounces voodoo lager,
   or any dark lager

½ pound butter, chopped

½ cup parsley, chopped

Process rosemary, pepper and seafood seasoning in a coffee grinder. In a large skillet melt 2 tablespoons butter. Add garlic and shrimp, stir, add 2 tablespoons spice mix and toss. Add Worcestershire and cook to reduce. Add beer and simmer. Reduce, remove shrimp and reduce further. Add remaining butter and incorporate. Pour over shrimp, garnish with parsley.

The *Arizona Daily Star* said, in a 2001 review of Pastiche, that eating at this eclectic American bistro was like eating at your best friend's house "if your best friend were an excellent chef and had a flair for interior decorating."

That sentiment still holds true today at Pat Connors' 8-year-old restaurant, where creative, exquisite dishes compete for your attention with dazzling works from local artists and attentive, intelligent service.

Pastiche
Modern Eatery

Pastiche
modern eatery

Pastiche Modern Eatery

3025 N Campbell Avenue
325-3333
Serving Lunch, Dinner
and Late Night
$$-$$$

Pat Connors, a mathematician by training and "foodie" by passion, has operated Pastiche since 1998. He and his wife, Julie, co-own the restaurant along with the newly opened addition, the Pastiche Wine Shop, where you can purchase gourmet cheeses, Certified Angus Beef® and a nearly unlimited choice of wine.

"Pastiche" is a word meaning a collage, or a unique collection, made up of bits and pieces from several different works. Given the restaurant's bold American cuisine, the name is extremely fitting. Connors describes the restaurant as eclectic American, which, to him, is a license to open just about any culinary door and play. With tenured chef Don Kishensky at the helm, Connors is doing just that. Consider these delectable possibilities: Mushroom Soufflé Topped with Asiago Cream Sauce; Baby Green Salad with Sliced Green Apples, Seasoned Walnuts, Blue Cheese and Orange Vinaigrette Dressing; Voodoo Cajun Pasta that pairs Grilled Chicken, Shrimp and Andouille Sausage with a slightly spicy New Orleans's Creole; Thyme Crusted Seabass served on Smoked Tomatoes and Capers Beurre Blanc with a tantalizing Champagne Cream Sauce. Pastry chef Lorraine Glicksman adds wondrous treats like Semi-flourless Brownies, Ginger Molasses Cake and Banana Bread Pudding.

While food and wine is their focus, the Connors' hearts have always been squarely centered on helping others. They and their 8-year-old son, Cole, volunteer monthly to serve food at the Primavera Foundation's Men's Shelter. "I want to set a good example for my son." said Connors. "I don't want him to think that because someone is down on his luck you have to ignore him. You can help. I want him to see that."

Connors was largely responsible for the collaboration between Primavera and the Tucson Originals. He contributed to the 2000 "Tucson Cooks!" cookbook and recruited fellow restaurant owners the following year for the Primavera Cooks! fundraisers. "I'm very lucky to be so young and have a restaurant and be able to do what I do," he said. "I'm not here to just take the money and run with it. I'm part of the community. I want Tucson to grow and be healthy."

Pastiche Modern Eatery
August 2002

EXECUTIVE CHEF

Don Kishensky

APPRENTICE CHEFS

Dee and Leslie Cohen
Lorraine Freyer
Karla Weeks
Jon Young

"It was hot and steamy but the high energy carried us through."
~Dee and Leslie Cohen

"I was surprised how quickly every- thing is cooked and how beautifully organized everyone is."
~Lorraine Freyer

First Course Assorted Bruschettas • Robert Mondavi Fumé Blanc

Second Course Don's Famous Gazpacho • Byron Chardonnay

Third Course Traditional Caesar Salad with House Smoked Salmon and Parmesan Cheese Crisps • La Famiglia di Robert Mondavi Barbera

Fourth Course Grilled Lamb Chops with Garlic Balsamic Glaze, served with Broiled Tomato, Almond Haricot Verts, and Mashed Root Vegetables • La Vite Lucente IGT (Sangiovese-Merlot Blend)

Fifth Course Sacher Torte (one of Europe's most famous desserts) • La Famiglia di Robert Mondavi Moscato Bianco

Left to right: Leslie Cohen, Don Kishensky, Jon Young, Lorraine Freyer, Carla Weeks, Dee Cohen and staff

Don's Famous Gazpacho

INGREDIENTS

Gazpacho

1 onion, diced
1 can tomatoes, diced
3 fresh tomatoes
1 green peppers
1 cucumber
2 cups fresh sourdough bread
1 cup tomato juice
½ cup parsley, diced
1 cup red wine vinegar
1 teaspoon cumin
salt and pepper to taste
1 cup olive oil

Place all ingredients in a blender. Blend until smooth consistency. Yield is 6–8 cups and is best served chilled.

Tuna Olive Tapénade and Sun-dried Tomato Cream Cheese Spread

INGREDIENTS

Tapénade

1 can tuna, drained
1 dozen kalamata olives
2 anchovies
6 capers
3 teaspoons olive oil
salt and pepper, to taste

Cheese Spread

1 cup sun-dried tomatoes
10 cloves roasted garlic
¾ pound cream cheese
salt and pepper to taste
hot water

For Tapénade Put all ingredients in food processor and blend until a smooth consistency. Spread on toasted slices of sourdough baguettes to a desired thickness.

For Spread Soak sun-dried tomatoes in hot water for ½ hour (to rehydrate). Put all ingredients in food processor and blend until a smooth consistency. Spread on toasted slices of sourdough baguettes to a desired thickness.

For Bruschetta Slice sourdough loaf on a slight bias. Brush bread slices with melted butter. Place on a sheet pan and bake at 350° for 7-10 minutes. Check after 5 minutes to avoid over cooking the toast.

Pastiche Modern Eatery
May 2003

EXECUTIVE CHEF

Don Kishensky

APPRENTICE CHEFS

Kermit Austin
Richard Weeks
Jon Young

"Great staff and this kitchen is a well oiled machine." ~Richard Weeks

"Simplicity is the key to flavor." ~Kermit Austin

First Course House Smoked Salmon Wrapped Around Goat Cheese and Asparagus Tips, Crab Sushi Rolls, Steak Tartar, and Falafel Stics • Ecco Domani Maso Canali Pinot Grigio

Second Course Steamed Manilla Clams with Tomato Concasse, Fresh Garlic, and Parsley • Frei Brothers Reserve Chardonnay

Third Course Sliced Roasted Duck with Fresh Blackberries over Arugala Greens with a Light Walnut Oil Vinaigrette • MacMurray Pinot Noir

Fourth Course Tucson Mixed Grill: Grilled Lamb Chops with Garlic Balsamic Glaze, Grilled Fillet Mignon with Chimichurri Sauce, Gourmet Sausage with Whole Grain Mustard Honey Served with a Napoleon of Root Vegetables • Marcelina Cabernet Sauvignon

Fifth Course Apple Crepes with Melted Brie • Anapamu Riesling

Left to right: Richard Weeks, Anthony Ortiz, Kermit Austin, Pat Connors, Jon Young, and Don Kishensky

Grilled Lamb Chops with Garlic Balsamic Glaze

INGREDIENTS

Lamb Chops

2 lamb racks, frenched
6 cloves garlic, chopped fine
2 sprigs fresh rosemary, destemmed
½ cup olive oil
1 teaspoon black pepper

Glaze

2 teaspoon olive oil
15 cloves garlic roughly chopped
2 cups balsamic vinegar
½ cup brown sugar
2 cups demi-glaze (brown sauce)
Cornstarch/water mixture (to thicken)

For Lamb Chops Cut lamb into double chops. Marinate in chopped garlic, rosemary, olive oil and black pepper. Grill over coals. Season with salt while grilling. Cook to deisred temperature.

For Glaze Add garlic and a little olive oil to a sauté pot . Brown the garlic but do not burn it. Add balsamic vinegar and reduce by half. Add brown sugar and demi-glaze. Thicken with cornstarch mixture if necessary. Strain the sauce through a sieve or colander.

Apple Crepes with Melted Brie

INGREDIENTS

Crepes

1 cup flour
¼ cup lukewarm water
½ cup milk
2 large eggs
2 tablespoons butter melted
1 tablespoon sugar

Filling

4 thinly sliced and peeled
   Granny Smith apples
2 tablespoons butter
2 tablespoons brown sugar
1 pound Brie

For Crepes Mix all ingredients together, place in a container. Cover with plastic wrap for 1 hour. Pour small amount of vegetable oil on a non-stick pan. Set heat to medium. Stir batter, pour small amount (2 tablespoons) into pan, lift off the heat and swirl batter to make a thin even layer. Turn crepe over and cook until browned.

For Filling Sauté thinly sliced apples with butter and a dash of brown sugar. Place in corner of crepe with thinly sliced ripe Brie. Fold into 4 to make a triangle shape.

Store-bought ready-made crepes work well and save a lot of time.

Pastiche Modern Eatery
August 2004

EXECUTIVE CHEF

Don Kishensky

APPRENTICE CHEFS

Megan Thompson
Karla and Richard Weeks
Karen Young
Tracy Goode

"When you see the final product of food plated so perfectly you really feel a sense of accomplishment."
~Megan Thompson

"This is the best charity event I have ever been involved in."
~Karla Weeks

First Course Passed Hors d'oeurves, Tuna Tartare, Savory Mini Chicken Skewers, Baked Brie and Fruit in Puff Pastry • Maso Canali Pinot Grigio

Second Course Chilled Vichyssoise with Chive Oil • McWilliams Hanwood Estate Chardonnay

Third Course Roasted Duck Breast on Mesclun Greens with Mushroom Pate and Hazelnut-Orange Vinaigrette • MacMurray Pinot Noir

Fourth Course Whole Roasted Beef Tenderloin, Marinated in Fresh Herbs and Garlic served with Au Jus and Assorted Baby Root Vegetables and Sautéed Spinach with White Truffle Oil • Louis M. Martini Reserve Cabernet Sauvignon

Fifth Course Chocolate Crème Brulée Napoleon with Hazelnut Crunch • Rancho Zabaco Reserve Zinfandel

Left to right: Richard Weeks, Karla Weeks, Megan Thompson, Karen Young, and Tracy Goode

Roasted Duck with Fresh Blackberries over Arugula Greens with Walnut Oil Vinaigrette

INGREDIENTS

Duck

duck breast, trimmed
Kosher salt
fresh cracked pepper
fresh arugula
fresh blackberries

Vinaigrette

1 tablespoon Dijon mustard
3 tablespoons red wine vinegar
½ cup walnut oil
salt and pepper

For Duck Season duck breast with salt and fresh pepper to taste. Sear fat side down until skin is caramelized and has a nice golden brown color. Place in a roasting pan skin side up and roast in a hot oven 450° for approximately 7 minutes or until medium rare. Slice into 7-8 thin slices. Place on dressed arugula and place 5-7 fresh blackberries on top.

For Vinaigrette Place mustard and vinegar in a mixing bowl. While whisking, slowly pour in ½ cup walnut oil. Season with salt and pepper to taste.

Vichyssoise with Chive Oil

INGREDIENTS

Vichyssoise

3 large baking potatoes
3 large leeks (mostly white parts
  and a little green)
8 cups chicken stock
1 pint heavy cream
½ teaspoon white pepper
chive oil

Chive Oil

1 bunch chives or green onions
½ cup chopped parsley
½ cup chopped fresh basil
1 cup light olive oil

For Vichyssoise In a large pot, place cut potatoes and leeks in chicken stock and boil until very soft. Chill. Place in food processor or blender and pure with cream, a little at a time. Add white pepper. Keep chilled and serve in cold bowls. Drizzle with chive oil.

For Oil In a large pot of salted boiling water, place green ingredients for 20 seconds. Pour through strainer and chill immediately in ice water using the strainer. Place in blender and slowly pour in oil while blending. Place in squeeze bottle for drizzling.

Pastiche Modern Eatery
June 2005

EXECUTIVE CHEF

Don Kishensky

APPRENTICE CHEFS

Megan Thompson
Karla Weeks
Karen and Jon Young

" Being an apprentice is not for the faint of heart! It's the hardest job I've ever loved." ~Karla Weeks

" I couldn't believe there were so many dirty pots." ~Jon Young

First Course Bread Spreads: Roasted Garlic, Herbed Goat Cheese, Tuna Tapénade with sliced French Baguettes • Kenwood Yalupa Cuvée Brut

Second Course Bacon Wrapped Escargot served in Puff Pastry with Béarnaise Sauce • Lake Sonoma Winery Fumé Blanc

Third Course Baked Brie breaded with Toasted Hazelnuts, served with Mixed Greens and Honey Raspberry Vinaigrette • Kenwood Pinot Noir

Fourth Course Seared Duck Breast with Cherry Demi-Glace, served with Silky Smooth Saffron Whipped Yukon Gold Potatoes, Haricots Verts and Glazed Baby Carrots • Valley of the Moon Cuvee de la Luna Cabernet Sauvignon Cabernet Franc Petit Verdot Merlot

Fifth Course Midnight Truffle Cake, a Black Cocoa Sponge Cake Layered with Rosettes of Chocolate Sour Cream Icing and Topped with Chocolate Truffles • Kenwood Jack London Vineyard Zinfandel

Left to right: Megan Thompson, Don Kishensky, Karla Weeks, Lorraine Glicksma Jon Young, and Anthony Ortiz

Bacon Wrapped Escargot in Puff Pastry with Béarnaise Sauce

INGREDIENTS

Escargot in Puff Pastry

12–15 slices of bacon
2–3 sheets of puff pastry
20–30 large canned escargots
3–4 egg yolks

Béarnaise Sauce

6 large eggs
½ pound warm (not hot)
  clarified butter
3 teaspoons lemon juice
3 teaspoons white wine
3 teaspoons white wine vinegar
leaves from 6 tarragon sprigs
1 teaspoon Tabasco sauce
1 teaspoon Worcestershire sauce
salt and pepper to taste

For Escargot in Puff Pastry Lay sliced bacon on sheet tray. Set oven at 400°. Place tray in oven and bake for 12–15 minutes or until crispy. Remove tray from oven and place bacon on paper towels to cool off. Cut bacon into 1" strips. In a small bowl whip yolks to a nice smooth texture. Cut puff pastry into 2"x 2" squares. Place one escargot and one piece of bacon in the middle of each puff pastry square. Fold pastry around contents and brush the outside of each pastry with whipped egg yolk. Spray a clean sheet tray with an oil base pan coating. Place pastries 1 inch apart on tray. Bake at 400° for 15–20 minutes or until outside of puff pastry is golden brown. Remove from oven, drizzle with béarnaise sauce and serve.

For Sauce In stainless steel bowl, combine egg yolks and wine. Place on top of pot with boiling water, whisk until egg mixture starts to stiffen. Be careful not to let egg yolks overcook. Remove from heat. Slowly add clarified butter a little at a time and whisk in rapidly. Continue until butter is added completely and the mixture is stiff. Add tarragon and remaining ingredients to the mixture. Season with salt and pepper to taste.

Saffron Whipped Yukon Gold Potatoes

INGREDIENTS

Potatoes

6–8 medium Yukon gold potatoes
  (peeled and cut into quarters)
½ pound butter (cut in ½" squares)
2 cups heavy cream
1 teaspoon saffron
  (placed in ¼ cup of water)
salt and white pepper to taste

Add potatoes to a pot of boiling water. Cook until potatoes are tender. Remove from heat and drain water through a strainer. Place potatoes in a large mixing bowl and begin to mash. For a nicer and fluffier texture, push potatoes through a potato ricer. Add remaining ingredients and season to taste.

Terra Cotta has been a member of Tucson Originals since the organization's founding, and Don Luria was the founding president. In both 2002 and 2004 the restaurant participated in the Primavera Cooks! Event. Terra Cotta has a fine reputation as a strong supporter of the Tucson Culinary and Art communities.

Terra Cotta

Terra Cotta

3500 E Sunrise Drive
577-8100
Serving Lunch and Dinner
$$$-$$$$

Terra Cotta is on the verge of celebrating both its 20th anniversary and its first anniversary. Confused? In 1986, the chic Southwestern Café Terra Cotta opened, bathed in cool desert hues, and began serving rich, elegant dishes using the best of fresh regional ingredients. Executive chef/owner Donna Nordin prepared dishes with French sensibilities she learned in France — the same techniques she had used to trained fledgling chefs in classes and seminars nationwide. Quickly Café Terra Cotta became renowned for it innovative Southwestern fare, lovely atmosphere and fine service.

In July 2004, a fire nearly destroyed the dream of Nordin and her co-owner husband Don Luria. The restaurant was seriously damaged. Determined not to let their fine dining establishment disappear, Luria and Nordin busied themselves rebuilding and restoring the beautiful space; from the desert color scheme accentuated by fine Southwestern artists to the copper bar in the center of the dining room.

The restaurant reopened in January 2005, with its simpler new name, Terra Cotta, and a new menu. But the old philosophy remains true: employ the best and freshest regional ingredients in innovative dishes "kissed" with passion and creativity. The end result is delights such as duck, sweet and moist, paired with a spicy-sweet Ancho-plum chutney; pizzas, cooked in a wood-burning oven visible from the dining room; Goat Cheese Stuffed Prawns, and Chicken Scaloppini. Chef Nordin's specialty is desserts and they are decadent and innovative: Chocolate Angel Food Cake Sundae, Pecan Cheesecake and Mark's Ice Box Parfait, which is sure to bring back memories of days gone by with its perfect balance of banana and chocolate puddings.

Terra Cotta
July 2002

EXECUTIVE CHEFS

Donna Nordin
Matthew Lash

APPRENTICE CHEFS

Lupita Murillo and
husband Don Gutzler

"It's like a ballet." ~Don Gutzler

"I taught the chef a thing or two."
~Lupita Murrillo

First Course Hors d'oeuvres by Lupita served with Don Gutzler's Secret Margarita Recipe, Sopa de Elote y Poblano (Corn and Poblano Soup) • Sonoita Vineyards Sauvignon Blanc

Second Course Ensalada de Nopalitos (Cactus Paddle Salad) • Montes "Barrel Fermented" Reserve Chardonnay

Third Course Pollo Encilantrada (Chicken and Tomatillo Enchiladas) • Pesquera

Fourth Course Puerco con Margarita (Pork Fillet in Tequila Cilantro Sauce) • Faustino I Gran Reserva, Rioja

Fifth Course Lupita's Banana Rum Cake • Chateau Camou "Flor de Guadalupe" Zinfandel

Left to right: Don Luria, Lupita Murillo, Don Gutzler, and Donna Nordin

Sopa de Elote y Poblano (Corn and Poblano Soup)

Sopa de Elote y Poblano

2 quarts milk

2 tablespoons cumin seeds

2 bay leaves

1 sprig of fresh rosemary
  or ½ teaspoon, dried

¼ cup olive oil or 4 tablespoons
  unsalted butter

2 large onions, diced

2 teaspoons salt

4-6 garlic cloves, minced

2 teaspoons cumin, ground

8 cups fresh or canned
  whole kernel corn

6 Poblano chilies, roasted,
  peeled, seeded and diced

1 bunch chives, thinly sliced
  for garnish

Combine milk, cumin seeds, bay leaves and rosemary in medium saucepan. Place over low heat and bring nearly to a simmer. (Do not boil). Remove from heat and let sit for 20 minutes. Heat olive oil in a large saucepan or stockpot over medium heat. Add onions with salt, cumin and garlic; cook for 5 minutes until golden brown, stirring frequently. Stir in corn and diced chiles: continue cooking over low heat for 5 more minutes. Using a fine strainer, strain the infused milk into the corn and chile mixture. Bring to a very slow simmer over low heat. Simmer gently for 15 minutes. Pour ⅓ of the soup into a food processor or blender and purée; stir back into soup pot. Serve hot in shallow soup bowls. Garnish with chives.

Ensalada de Nopalitos (Cactus Paddle Salad)

Ensalada de Nopalitos

12-15 fresh cactus paddles

3 tablespoons olive oil

2 tablespoons lime juice

1 clove garlic, minced

6 scallions, chopped

2 large tomatoes, peeled,
  seeded and chopped

¼ cup cilantro, chopped

1 jalapeño or Serrano chile,
  seeded and chopped

salt and pepper

Trim off outside edges of paddles and any stickers. Cut into ¾ inch strips. Place them on a baking sheet in a single layer with a little oil, salt and pepper. Roast in a 450-475° oven for about 20 minutes on top rack; remove from oven and let cool.

Whisk the lime juice, garlic and olive oil together in a large mixing bowl. Add cactus paddles, scallions, tomatoes, cilantro and chile. Season to taste with salt and pepper. Toss well and chill for at least 1 hour.

Terra Cotta
June 2004

EXECUTIVE CHEF

Chef Tom Mead

APPRENTICE CHEFS

Shirley Chann

Shirley and Maurice Sevigny

First Course A Selection East Meets West Hors d'oeuvres: Vietnamese Fresh Spring Rolls, Asian Shrimp Skewers, Southwestern BBQ Ribs • Valley of the Moon Pinot Blanc

Second Course Shirley Chann's Spicy Black Mussels with Rice Stick Noodles • Lake Sonoma Fume Blanc

Third Course Maurice's Southwestern Duck à la Orange with Lemon Grass Bok Choy and Black Sticky Rice • Kenwood Jack London Vineyard Merlot

Fourth Course A Shirley, Shirley and Maurice Collaboration of Profiteroles with Coconut Ice Cream, Chocolate Sauce and Fresh Berries • Lake Sonoma Dry Creek Zinfandel

"I was surprised to see how many people it takes to pull off something like this." ~Shirley Sevigny

"Those who can afford to eat out need to support those who can't." ~Maurice Sevigny

Left to right: Shirley Chann, Don Luria, Shirley Sevigny, Maurice Sevigny, and Tom Mead

Asian Shrimp Skewers

INGREDIENTS

Asian Shrimp Skewers

large shrimp peeled and deveined
½ cup soy sauce
¼ cup lemon juice
1 tablespoon ginger, chopped
1 tablespoon garlic, chopped
½ bunch scallions, sliced
2 tablespoons sesame oil
½ cup salad oil

Add soy sauce, lemon juice, ginger, garlic, and scallions to a mixing bowl. Slowly whisk in sesame and salad oil. Marinate shrimp for 30 minutes and then cook on grill for about 5-10 minutes. Place shrimp on bamboo skewers and serve.

Maurice's Southwestern Duck à la Orange with Lemon Grass Bok Choy and Black Sticky Rice

INGREDIENTS

Duck à la Orange

1 duck breast split
1 teaspoon chili powder
¼ cup grand marnier
¼ cup orange juice

Bok Choy

1 baby bok choy
1 lemon grass stalk

Sticky Rice

1 cup black rice (available
*   at most Asian markets)*
4 cup water
1 tablespoon rice wine vinegar
1 teaspoon sugar

For Duck à la Orange Sauté duck breast skin side down for about 5 minutes over a medium heat. Turn duck over and add chili powder, Grand Marnier, and orange juice. Place sauté pan in the oven at 350° for about 5-7 minutes.

For bok choy Add lemon grass to pot of water. Boil for about 10 minutes. Blanch the bok choy for 2 minutes. Remove and set aside until ready to serve.

For rice Boil the rice in a covered pan for 30 minutes; strain excess water off. Stir in the rice wine vinegar and sugar.

Other Tucson Restaurants

The following restaurants are Tucson Originals
sharing some of their best recipes.

*Tucson chef Albert Hall started his new culinary adventure last fall when
he opened Acacia, located in St. Philip's Plaza. Acacia serves inspired, upscale
fare including pan-seared diver scallops with a pink grapefruit vinaigrette
as an appetizer and an assortment of chops, steaks, seafood, and poultry
entrees. Desserts will bowl you over, from hand-crafted ice cream to a
chocolate toffee and gingersnap cheesecake.*

Acacia

4340 N Campbell Avenue
232-0101
Serving Lunch, Dinner,
Late Night and Sunday
Brunch
$$$$

Chipotle Molasses Glazed Rotisserie Chicken

INGREDIENTS

Chicken

3 whole fryers, 2 ¾ -3 pounds each
3 tablespoons Embassa brand chipotle
  in adobo, puréed
2 cups Blackstrap Molasses
8 ounces tomato sauce
5 cloves crushed garlic
¼ cup red wine vinegar
4½ cups mirepoix (2 parts onion,
  one part carrot and one part celery
  chopped into ½" pieces)
2 teaspoons fresh thyme chopped
salt and pepper to taste

In a stainless steel bowl, combine puréed chipotle, molasses, tomato sauce, crushed garlic and vinegar. Whisk. Let stand at room temperature for two hours. Rinse fryers in cold water. Blot dry with paper towels. Rub cavity of each bird with salt and pepper then fill with mirepoix. Separate skin from breasts without tearing. Use your fingers to rub the pockets with fresh thyme, salt and pepper. Truss birds and skewer according to manufacturer's directions. Roast over medium heat for 1-1½ hours basting birds with the chipotle-molasses glaze for the last 15 minutes coating evenly as they continue to cook. If grill flares up, the glaze will burn. When well caramelized, remove from fire. Let stand 15-20 minutes before removing from skewer. Snip the twine and split birds in half. Remove mirepoix, backbone, breastbone and rib bones. Serve in ½ chicken portions.

Apricot, Honey Mustard Glazed Pork Loin

INGREDIENTS

Pork Loin

1, 8-bone center cut pork rack
1, 12-ounce jar apricot preserves,
  puréed
1 teaspoon garlic, chopped
½ cup whole grain Dijon mustard
¼ cup honey
4 jalapeños, seeded, ribbed
  and minced
¼ cup red wine vinegar
3 tablespoons cilantro, chopped
salt and pepper

For Glaze Whisk all ingredients together in a stainless steel bowl until well incorporated. Store refrigerated for up to 1 week.

For Pork Order a center cut frenched 8-bone pork rack. Tear a piece of foil twice the length of roast and fold in half lengthwise, then fold over the bones and crimp. Tie roast in between each bone with butchers twine. Skewer the pork by running rod about an inch above where eye of the roast and the bone meet. Run the skewer along rib bones the length of the roast. The roast should be somewhat balanced on skewer. Secure with prongs and tighten thumbscrews. Season with salt and pepper to taste. Cook on rotisserie for 40-50 minutes over medium heat or until 135-140°. Begin basting with glaze. Continue until well caramelized. Pork should still be pink, medium to medium well. Remove from rotisserie and let stand in a warm place for 15-20 minutes. Serve with remaining glaze.

In its almost decade of existence, this intimate bistro has become a downtown destination. It's the spot for late-night diners, hoping to indulge in more than a burger or nachos following a night of theater or music. Barrio dishes up to-die-for fish tacos and a tempting house chicken pasta that's dressed in a poblano chili-kissed sauce. Ancho chilies infuse a kick in the aioli, dressing a pan-fried barbecued venison.

Barrio Food & Drink

135 S Sixth Avenue
629-0191
Serving Lunch, Dinner,
Late Night
$$$

Shrimp, Crab, Bacon, Saffron Jerk Bisque

INGREDIENTS

Jerk Bisque

¼ pound unsalted butter

½ cup carrot, minced

½ cup celery, minced

½ cup yellow onion, minced

¼ cup fresh garlic, minced

2 cups Chardonnay

2 tablespoon lobster base

2 tablespoons Jamaican jerk spice

1 teaspoon saffron, crushed

½ cup cooked bacon, diced

1 gallon heavy cream

½ cup Brie diced

1 cup crabmeat

2 cups shrimp, diced

sea salt

¼ cup lemon juice

¼ cup mixed herbs, minced

Sauté carrots, celery, onion and garlic in butter until translucent. Add white wine, lobster base, jerk spice and saffron. Reduce by half. Add bacon and cream. Reduce by half. Add Brie, crab, shrimp, salt, to taste, lemon juice and herbs.

Mango Pasta

INGREDIENTS

Mango Pasta

4 tablespoons shallots, diced

2 teaspoons garlic, minced

2 cups chicken breast, grilled and diced

14 ounces dried mango, diced

14 ounces dried papaya, diced

1 cup dry white wine

4 cups heavy cream

1 teaspoon chipotle pepper, diced

1 tablespoon fresh lemon juice

salt and pepper

In large pan with oil, sauté the shallots and garlic until translucent. Add chicken and dried fruit, and stir. Deglaze the pan with white wine and reduce by half. Add heavy cream and reduce by half again. Add chipotle, lemon juice and salt and pepper to taste. Toss with your favorite precooked pasta.

Old West accents make a night out at Chad's a walk through history.
But the motif will be all but forgotten once you dig into a piping slab of
Black Angus prime rib or savor that first bite into a melt-in-your-mouth
silky rib eye. The sirloin burgers here are unforgettable. Chad's with its
signature baked cheese bread has been a tradition for 13 years.

Chad's Steakhouse & Saloon

3001 N Swan Road
881-1802
Serving Lunch and Dinner
$$

Chad's Cowboy Beans

INGREDIENTS

Beans

1 quart pinto beans

1, 6-ounce can green chilies, diced

1/8 cup salt

1/8 cup chili powder

2 tablespoons salt and pepper

2 tablespoons granulated garlic

1/4 teaspoon cajun spice

2 quarts au jus

4 quarts water

In medium pot, add beans, and liquid. Bring beans to a boil, set to medium, and cook beans until soft (approximately 1½-2 hours). Add in spices along the way and stir frequently. Enjoy!

Chad's Famous Blue Cheese Salad Dressing

INGREDIENTS

Salad Dressing

1 pound blue cheese crumbles

1/2 gallon buttermilk

2 pounds sour cream

1/4 cup Worcestershire

2 ounces hot sauce (Gunslinger)

2 tablespoon granulated garlic

pinch cayenne pepper

6 pounds mayonnaise

Mix together well cheese, milk cream, sauces, garlic and pepper. Be sure sour cream is broken down. Add mayonnaise and whisk thoroughly—leave no mayo chunks. Enjoy!

For the better part of almost two decades, Dakota Café has been a pleasant jolt of sophistication in the shorts-and-T-shirt casualness of Trail Dust Town. The quesadilla appetizer eschews traditional Cheddar or jack cheese and grilled meat for the untraditional and refreshing Brie and fresh mango. On the dinner menu, grilled rack of lamb vies for your attention over braised short ribs and a pistachio jalapeño-crusted salmon dish.

Dakota Café
& Catering

6541 E Tanque Verde Road
298-7188
Serving Lunch and Dinner
Closed Sunday
$$$

White Chicken Enchiladas

INGREDIENTS

Enchiladas

2½ pounds boiled/shredded chicken
½ chopped onion sautéed
   in 2 tablespoons butter
¾ cups chopped green chilies
¾ cup chopped tomato
1 teaspoon chopped garlic
1 teaspoon cumin
½ teaspoon black pepper
½ teaspoon salt
2 cups tomatillo sauce
1 package flour tortillas
1½ cups sour cream mixed
   with ½ cup milk
3 cups shredded mixed jack
   and cheddar cheese

Sauté chicken, onion, chilies, tomato and garlic with cumin, pepper and salt for 5 minutes. Layer ⅓ tomatillo sauce, ⅓ of tortillas, ⅓ of chicken mixture, ⅓ of sour cream mixture and ⅓ of cheese in a 9x12 pan. Repeat—ending with cheese on top. Bake at 350° for 45-50 minutes or until top is golden brown.

Corn Baked Casserole

INGREDIENTS

Casserole

½ cup diced onion
½ cup chopped green chilies
½ cup butter
1, 16-ounce can whole kernel
   corn with liquid
1, 16-ounce can creamed corn
2 cups Jiffy corn meal
4 eggs
1 cup sour cream
16 ounces shredded mixed jack
   and cheddar cheese

Sauté onions and chilies in butter. Add remaining ingredients and pour into greased 9x12 pan. Bake at 350° for 45-50 minutes.

Culinary worlds have collided for 20 years in this East Side dining room, where American and Mexican fare share the spotlight with tempting pasta dishes. Many of the dishes on all sides of the menu are vegetarian friendly.

Eclectic Café

7053 E. Tanque Verde Road
885-2842
Serving Lunch and Dinner
Breakfast on Saturday
and Sunday
$$

Chicken and Chorizo with Roasted Red Peppers and Artichoke Hearts on Penne Pasta

INGREDIENTS

Chicken and Chorizo
with Pasta

1 pound chorizo

1 quart heavy cream

½ teaspoon cumin

4 jalapeños, diced

chicken base to taste

red and green peppers diced

green onions, diced

tomatoes, diced

olives

artichoke hearts

1 whole boneless chicken breast,
    grilled and sliced

Parmesan cheese

parsley

In large skillet, cook chorizo. Add all other ingredients. Serve over penne pasta. Top with Parmesan cheese and chopped parsley if desired.

Tahini Eggplant Salad with Mesquite Bacon

INGREDIENTS

Eggplant Salad

8 slices bacon, grilled crisp
    and set aside

1 whole large eggplant,
    peeled and diced

1 medium onion, peeled and chopped

2 medium tomatoes, diced

2 tablespoons sweet basil, dried

5 ounces tahini (hulled sesame butter)

fresh spinach leaves, washed

1 boiled egg, chopped

cucumber, sliced

sunflower sprouts

Grill together eggplant, onion, tomatoes and basil with olive oil. When mix sweats add chopped bacon and tahini. Continue to grill for a few more minutes.

Serve over fresh spinach leaves and add, egg and cucumber. Top with sunflower sprouts and serve with your choice of sweet dressing.

El Charro opened in 1922 and has never closed nor changed owners, making it the country's oldest, continuously operated Mexican food restaurant. In the past couple of years, the family-owned eatery specializing in authentic Sonoran cuisine and killer sun-dried carne seca, has been on an expansion crusade, opening satellite restaurants on the north side of town and a centrally located spot on bustling East Speedway and Swan.

El Charro Café

311 N Court Avenue
622-1922

6310 E Broadway
745-1922

100 W Orange Grove
615-1922

4699 E Speedway
325-1922

Serving Lunch and Dinner
$$-$$$

Sopa de Tortilla (Tortilla Soup)

INGREDIENTS

Sopa

6 cups chicken broth, skimmed

1 tablespoon oil

1 cup white onion, chopped

1 bell pepper, chopped

2 cups tomatoes, chopped

2 cups green chilies, chopped

1 tablespoon garlic purée

1 tablespoon oregano

1 tablespoon peeper

2 tablespoons seasoning salt, optional

6 small corn tortillas, cut lengthwise
   and fried until crisp

1 cup shredded white cheese
   (such as Monterey Jack)

1 avocado, pitted, peeled and diced

½ cup green onion, chopped,
   green part only

1 tablespoon cilantro chopped, optional

Tortilla soup can be a light appetizer or a filling meal. El Charro Café serves tortillas soup in a thick, earthenware pots; it comes garnished with crisp tortilla chips, slivers of fresh avocado and a light sprinkle of Mexican cheese. In a large pot bring the broth to a boil; reduce the heat to simmer. In a saucepan heat the oil and sauté the onion, bell peppers, tomatoes, green chilies and garlic purée until lightly translucent. Add to the simmering broth oregano, pepper and seasoning salt. Cover the pot and simmer for 20 minutes.

To Serve In each bowl, place ⅓ cup of cheese, add the broth and ⅙ of the diced avocado. Garnish with the green onions, the cilantro and float tortillas strips on top. For a heartier meal, add a cup of cooked, shredded chicken before serving.

Salsa de Chile Colorado (Red Enchilada Sauce)

INGREDIENTS

Salsa

12 dried red chilies

2 quarts of water, boiling

3 tablespoons oil

¼ cup garlic purée

3 tablespoons flour

½ teaspoon salt (or to taste)

Rinse chilies in cold water and remove stems. Cook in boiling water until tender, about 15 minutes. Remove chilies and reserve for cooking liquid. Place a few of the chilies in a blender or food processor with ½ cup reserved liquid and blend to a paste. Remove to bowl. Repeat with remaining chilies. Heat oil in a large skillet. Add garlic purée and flour, stirring until flour browns. Add the chili paste, stirring constantly until it boils and thickens. Season with salt. Thin sauce slightly with cooking liquid. Makes two quarts.

Celebrated Tucson restaurateur Daniel Scordato launched Intermezzo three years ago as a less-expensive take on his upscale Italian eatery Vivace. The restaurant quickly drew a fan base for its simple yet decadent manicotti topped with house marinara and selection of authentic Tuscan style Italian dishes. Last December, Scordato sold the business to Charlie and Stephanie Heckman, who've been keeping faithful to his mission.

Intermezzo

5350 E Broadway
748-8100
Serving Lunch, Dinner and
Sunday Brunch
$$-$$$

Bistro Fillet Salad with Strawberry-Balsamic Dressing

INGREDIENTS

Dressing

4 strawberries, sliced thin
1 ounce balsamic vinegar
2 ounces olive oil
1 teaspoon rubbed thyme
1 teaspoon fresh oregano
1 teaspoon salt
1 teaspoon black pepper
1 ½ cups organic seasonal greens
4 ounces bistro fillet or other
   tender, lean fillet
1 teaspoon blackening spice
1 tablespoon Romano cheese

Mix all spices and strawberries, cover with balsamic vinegar and let sit a few minutes. Add oil and sit in cool area until ready to use. Rub fillet with blackening spice and sear on all sides leaving meat rare. Let cool and slice into 1-ounce medallions. Arrange pieces around mixed greens and service plate. Add dressing and top with cheese.

Chai Crème Brûlée

INGREDIENTS

Crème Brûlée

½ gallon heavy cream
1 large vanilla bean
10 Chai tea bags
1 quart half and half
1 pound sugar
10 egg yolks

Pre-heat oven to 325°. Scald heavy cream with vanilla bean and chai tea bags. Remove from heat and add half and half to cool slightly. Add sugar and mix well. Add egg yolks and mix well. Strain through and place mixture in brûlée dishes. Bake dishes in hot water bath covered with foil that doesn't touch tops of brûlées. Bake 20-25 minutes or until center is set.

The casual, popular J BAR shares a building with Janos restaurant.
Janos Wilder is the owner of both J BAR and Janos. Southwest Regional Cuisine
is served in a lovely, bright red room with a bar, or on the rambling patio
that overlooks the city lights. J BAR features grilled marinated meats, ceviches,
quesadillas and other Mexican inspired creations. These are accompanied
by special salsas, hand stretched tortillas and a full line of boutique tequilas.
Produce from local gardeners and the freshest and finest ingredients make
this a delightful dining experience.

J BAR

3770 E Sunrise Drive
615-6100
Serving Dinner
Closed Monday
$$

Chihuacle Chile and Citrus-based Salmon with Roasted Tomatillo Salsa

INGREDIENTS

Marinade

1 Chihuacle negro chile, seeded
½ cup each lemon, lime
  and orange juice
½ cup honey
4, 7-ounce Norwegian salmon fillets
salt and pepper to taste

Salsa

1 pound tomatillos, husked and rinsed
2 Serrano chilies, seeded
½ medium white onion, sliced
  to ¼ inch thickness
3 cloves garlic, peeled
½ cup water
⅓ tablespoon salt
⅓ tablespoon sugar
⅓ cup cilantro, coarsely chopped

For Marinade Combine Chihuacle chile, citrus juice, and honey in a non-reactive pan and simmer until reduced by ⅔. Purée, strain and reserve. Grill salmon to desired temperature, basting with marinade. Arrange on 4 serving plates and pour remaining marinade over salmon.

For Salsa Broil Serrano chilies, onion and garlic on baking sheet until well browned. Purée tomatillos with water and sugar. Combine with chopped vegetables. Arrange mixture around and on top of salmon. Garnish with cilantro.

*European fingerprints are smudged throughout this quaint little bistro
where dining is a destination and eating is divine. Southern French
and northern Italian food is prepared with care and creativity, but not
to the point of stuffiness. Most of the dishes are swoonably simple and
down to earth.*

Livorno Country Bistro

5931 N Oracle Road
887-5171
Serving Dinner
Closed Monday
$$$

Chicken Livorno

INGREDIENTS

Chicken Livorno

*2–3 chicken breasts, boneless
and skinless, cut in half*

1–2 sage leaves

1–2 pieces of pancetta, thinly sliced

¼ cup extra virgin olive oil

1 teaspoon white wine

¼ cup heavy cream

1 tablespoon chicken stock/broth

small pat of butter

2–3 pieces caper berries or capers

½ teaspoon garlic

salt and pepper

Salt and pepper chicken on both sides to taste, add sage and top with pancetta. Heat sauté pan on high, add olive oil; when just smoking, add chicken breast pancetta side up. Brown chicken breasts, then turn down heat to medium, deglaze with white wine, add cream, chicken stock/broth, butter, capers and garlic.

Let reduce until sauce is nice and creamy or almost thick and chicken is done. If sauce cooks too quickly before chicken is done, add a little water until finished. Serve with rice, potatoes or pasta and your favorite fresh vegetables. Enjoy!

Bleu Cheese Fillet

INGREDIENTS

Fillet

*1–2 pieces beef fillet,
choice or higher*

*½ cup Stilton bleu cheese/Gorgonzola
or favorite bleu cheese*

¼ cup extra virgin olive oil

¼ cup heavy cream

¼ cup beef stock/broth

salt and pepper

Salt and pepper on both sides of fillet to taste. Add fillet to smoking hot sauté pan with olive oil, do not move fillet until it is nicely browned on one side. Turn, top with some bleu cheese, place under broiler till desired doneness and cheese is toasted golden brown. Remove fillet from pan, add cream, rest of bleu cheese and beef stock/broth, reduce until creamy smooth. Serve with fries and your favorite vegetable, top with sauce. Enjoy!

*Magpies Gourmet Pizza has consistently won every local survey as pizza lovers'
favorite pie for going on two decades. Chalk it up to the homegrown chain's
attention to detail. Pizza here is not just pepperoni and cheese plopped on
a generic dough. It's homegrown veggies, hand-grated cheese, freshly made
sausage and sauce carefully assembled on chewy, flavorful dough that stands
out as magnificently as the toppings.*

Magpies
Gourmet Pizza

605 N 4th Avenue
628-1661

105 S Houghton Road
751-9949

7315 N Oracle Road
297-2712

4654 E Speedway
795-5977

7157 E Tanque Verde Road
546-6526

Serving Lunch and Dinner
$-$$

Chicken Picante

INGREDIENTS

Chicken

1, 21-ounce ball of dough

1 tablespoon pesto sauce

¾ cup marinara sauce

¼ teaspoon jalapeño juice

⅓ cup feta cheese

⅔ cup lemon garlic chicken
   breast, roasted

1 sprig cilantro

2 tomatoes, sliced and halved

1½ cup mozzarella

Toss a 21-ounce dough ball into a 14" diameter pizza skin. This pizza skin is placed on a baking pan. On the skin put 1 tablespoon cup of pesto sauce, add ¼ teaspoon jalapeño juice and ½ cup marinara sauce, blend the sauces together in the middle of the skin. Use the back of a spoon to spread sauce out in a circle to ½" away from the edge of the crust.

Slice tomatoes and then cut the slices into half. Pull cilantro leaves off the stems. Dice the lemon roasted chicken. Crumble feta cheese. Shred 1½ cups of mozzarella cheese. Sprinkle 1 cup of mozzarella cheese over the sauce. Make sure to cover the sauce at the edge of the crust. A ½ inch crust should be left around the outside of the pizza skin. Leave the other ½ cup of mozzarella cheese for the very top of the pizza. Evenly sprinkle cilantro on top of the cheese. Place the halved tomato slices in even spaces around the pizza, to cover the whole area. Sprinkle the chicken in an even amount over the entire pizza. Drizzle the feta cheese in little clumps on the top of the other ingredients, avoiding the ½ crust area of the pizza. Now add the ½ cup of mozzarella to cover the top, again avoiding the ½" crust area of the pie. Preheat oven to 425°. Bake pizza for 12-16 minutes until crust is golden brown, vegetables are steamed, and cheese is golden brown. Let pizza stand for 5 minutes before cutting. Enjoy!

*Mama and family have been dishing up authentic Italian fare since 1956.
The restaurant has built its reputation by serving classic fare with family feel.
Menu favorites include Joe's Special, a signature dish (going on 50 years)
of homemade spaghetti topped by a special house cheese, hot pepper seeds, fresh
chopped garlic and the house famous sauce. Other favorites include several
linguine dishes with refreshingly simple olive oil and sliced garlic toppings
and homemade linguine.*

Mama Louisa's
Italian Restaurant

2041 S Craycroft Road
790-4702
Serving Lunch and Dinner
$$-$$$

Mama Louisa's Traditional Chicken Cacciatore

INGREDIENTS

Chicken Cacciatore

5 chickens, cleaned and cut into
  3 parts (leg, breast and thigh)
2 cups chopped garlic
2 tablespoons salt
2 teaspoons rosemary
2 tablespoons black pepper
½ cup olive oil
1 cup Chablis wine
1, 12-ounce can sliced mushrooms
1, 20-ounce can of tomato sauce
5 bell peppers, seeded and
  cut into quarters

In a large pan, brown garlic, salt, rosemary and pepper in oil. Add chicken to the same pan and cook until skin is brown and bone side is no longer pink. Remove and place in roasting pan, cover and cook in oven at 350° for 60 minutes. Add Chablis, mushrooms, tomato sauce and peppers to original pan and cook until peppers are soft and firm. Add chicken and serve.

Latin American cuisine dips into South America for dishes that will intrigue and thrill. Miguel's stands out as one of the city's more intriguing Mexican restaurants. An example: A tender grilled fillet of Mahi–Mahi is deglazed with tequila and topped with a Mexican cream sauce in the drunken fish. Yummo.

Miguel's

5900 N Oracle Road
837-7700
Serving Lunch and Dinner
$$$$

Seafood Relleno with Rice

INGREDIENTS

Seafood Relleno

½ cup rock shrimp

½ cup tilapia, cut into ½" cubes

½ cup albacore, cut into ½" cubes

½ cup bay scallops

2 tablespoons extra virgin olive oil

1 clove garlic

1 small white onion, finely chopped

2 tablespoons paprika

1 tablespoon Old Bay seasoning

¼ cup lemon juice, freshly squeezed

4 cups rice

¼ cup parsley, chopped

1 cup cheese mix (queso fresco,
    asadero and Chihuahua)

1 cup green onions, chopped

6-8 Poblano peppers

salt and pepper to taste

For Seafood In a large skillet heat olive oil and sauté garlic and white onion. Add all seafood and continue to cook for 2-3 minutes. While still on low heat add paprika, Old Bay seasoning and lemon juice. Cook for one more minute. Let cool. Save liquid for rice.

For Rice Rinse rice in cold water until clear. Cook rice in remaining liquid from seafood and let cool. Mix rice and seafood mixture and add parsley, cheese and green onion.

Roast Poblano peppers over low heat and place in a bowl and cover with plastic wrap. Let stand for 5 minutes. This will help to loosen skins. Peel and clean peppers. Stuff with mixture and top with cheese mix and reheat in a 350° oven for 5 minutes. Serve with your favorite side dish.

Capriotata

INGREDIENTS

Capriotata

10 cups leftover Danishes or croissants

½ cup dried cherries

½ cup dried cranberries

½ cup apricots

8 ounces mascarpone

4 cups half and half

1½ cups milk

1 cinnamon stick

2 teaspoon vanilla extract

1 piloncillo (size 3)

9 eggs

Toss together pastries, fruit and cheese and place in a greased and paper lined 10" pan. In medium pan heat milk and cream with seasonings and piloncillo until sugar dissolves. Strain out cinnamon stick. Temper in egg mixture and pour over bread mixture. Let set 10 minutes. Place in water bath and cover. Bake at 350° about 50-60 minutes or until set.

*Papagayo's has been a Mexican food mainstay for a quarter century,
boasting itself for dusting off authentic family recipes and employing
the freshest ingredients. In its heyday, Papagayo ran three locations.
Today, only its flagship remains.*

Papagayo Mexican Restaurant

4717 E Sunrise
577-6055
Serving Lunch and Dinner
$$-$$$

Papagayo's Almendrado

INGREDIENTS

Almendrado

1 teaspoon unflavored gelatin
3 tablespoons cold water
3 tablespoons boiling water
4 egg whites
¼ teaspoon cream of tartar
¾ cup sugar
1 teaspoon vanilla
1 teaspoon almond extract
1 teaspoon lemon rind, grated
few drops red food coloring
few drops green food coloring
⅓ cup sliced almonds

Lightly spray an 8x8 inch pan with nonstick cooking spray. In small bowl, sprinkle unflavored gelatin over cold water and mix; add boiling water and refrigerate. In mixing bowl, beat egg whites with cream of tartar until soft peaks start to form; add vanilla. Add almond extract and lemon rind, gradually beat in sugar. Beat mixture until stiff. Then beat in slightly thickened gelatin. Divide mixture into thirds, color ⅓ red (pink) another third green; add sliced almonds to remaining, uncolored third, reserving a few almond pieces for garnish. Spread green gelatin in pan; spread uncolored layer over that; finish with red layer. Top with reserved almonds. Refrigerate at least 30 minutes. To serve, cut into squares.

Green Corn Tamale Casserole

INGREDIENTS

Tamale Casserole

3 eggs, separated
1½ cups milk, scalded
1 cup white cornmeal
¾ teaspoon salt
¾ cup large curd cottage cheese
3 tablespoon butter
1, 17-ounce can of corn
   (white cream style)
1 teaspoon baking powder
½ pound longhorn cheese, grated
2, 8-ounce cans green chilies,
   cut into strips

Grease a 2-quart baking dish. In mixing bowl, beat egg whites (at room temperature) until stiff, but not dry. In separate bowl, beat yolks until thick and lemon colored. In medium pot, scald, stir in cornmeal and salt while beating hard. Cook a few seconds over low heat stirring until mixture is the consistency of thick mush. Blend in butter, corn, cottage cheese and finally baking powder. Fold in yolks, then whites. Pour into baking dish in layers of batter, grated cheese and chilies, last layer being batter. Bake in a 375° oven for 40 minutes or until fluffy golden brown.

A spacious patio with sprawling tables and jazz played live are trademarks of the 15-year-old Ric's Cafe. Eating outside is a Tucson passion, and at Ric's it's a pleasure to nibble on succulent steaks and fresh salads while a gentle breeze whistles a sweet melody.

Ric's Cafe

5605 E River Road
577-7272
Serving Lunch, Dinner
and Sunday Brunch
$$$

Ric's Cafe

Citrus Chipotle Vinaigrette

INGREDIENTS

Vinaigrette
2 ounces chipotle peppers
1½ cups fresh orange juice
½ cup red wine vinegar
4 ounces brown sugar
2 small garlic cloves
2 egg yolks
3–4 cups salad oil

Blend all ingredients together except the oil. Blend until smooth. Slowly add oil until vinaigrette is desired thickness. Refrigerate until chilled through. Use on any type of salad.

Jack's Famous Green Chili Chicken Soup

INGREDIENTS

Green Chili Chicken Soup
2 Anaheim peppers,
   roasted and seeded
2 red bell peppers,
   roasted and seeded
2 green bell peppers,
   roasted and seeded
4 medium chicken breasts,
   fat and gristle removed
2 red onions, diced
½ pound butter
½ cup all purpose flour
6 cups chicken stock
1 cup heavy cream or 2% milk
2 fresh jalapeños, seeded and
   finely chopped
salt and pepper

On a barbeque grill place the Anaheim peppers and bell peppers; roast until skin is blackened on both sides. Place peppers in a brown paper bag and seal. Let peppers cool 20 minutes. Season cleaned chicken with salt and pepper to taste. Spray chicken with nonstick spray. Cook chickens on a grill until cooked through, then place chicken in refrigerator to cool. Clean peppers in running water and peel off charred skin. Once clean, pull out seed pods and shake out extra seeds. Carefully dice peppers and onions. Place in a pot with the butter. Sauté until tender.

While peppers are cooking, cut chicken into bite-sized squares. When vegetables are tender, sprinkle in flour a little at a time so that lumps do not form. When all flour has been added, add chicken stock and cream (or milk) and bring to a boil. When soup boils, turn heat down to a simmer. Continue to stir until soup is slightly thickened. Add diced chicken. Salt and pepper to taste.

Cousins Rosa Holland and Gino Marinelli opened their storefront restaurant in 1983 as one of the Northwest Side's first bona fide Italian eateries. The restaurant serves up a mix of northern and southern Italian fare, specializing in tantalizing pastas and decadent veal and seafood dishes.

Roma Caffé

4140 W Ina Road
744-2929
Serving Lunch and Dinner
$$-$$$

Roma Caffé
Ristorante Italiano

Tomato Basil Bruschetta

INGREDIENTS

Bruschetta
4 slices rustic or artisan style bread
1 garlic clove
extra virgin olive oil
4 ripe tomatoes, diced
4 large basil leaves, thinly sliced
pinch of oregano
parmigliano or romano cheese, grated
salt to taste

Toast or grill slices of bread. Rub with garlic clove and drizzle with olive oil, set aside. In a mixing bowl add diced tomatoes and toss with a generous amount of olive oil, basil, salt and oregano. Sprinkle with grated cheese.

Penne all' Arrabiata
(Penne Pasta with Angry Sauce)

INGREDIENTS

Penne
1 pound penne pasta
3 tablespoons olive oil
2 garlic cloves, thinly sliced
4-6 medium red chilies, dried
6 large very ripe tomatoes,
  cut in small chunks
1 fresh basil leaf
Parmesan cheese, grated
salt

In a large skillet cook garlic and chilies until lightly brown but not crisp. Add tomatoes and salt to taste. Simmer, occasionally smashing down tomatoes while being careful not to break chilies. Cook for about 25 minutes or until desired thickness.

Cook pasta according to package directions to al dente, about 8-10 minutes. Drain pasta and place in a large serving bowl. Toss with ½ the sauce. Divide into 4 servings and top each serving with the remaining sauce. Top with grated cheese if desired.

Fresh Strawberries with Balsamic Vinegar

INGREDIENTS

Strawberries with Vinegar
1½ pound fresh strawberries
¾ cup balsamic vinegar
2½ tablespoons sugar
1 teaspoon lemon juice

Trim strawberries, slice into quarters and place in a bowl. In sauce pan, while stirring, heat vinegar, sugar and lemon juice, until sugar is dissolved. Cool. Toss berries with balsamic vinegar mixture. Chill for 1 hour. Delicious served over ice cream!

*For decades now, the special-night-out restaurant on the Northwest Side
has been the elegant, scene-stealing Gold Room. Elegance rules the day here,
where special touches elevate dinner out to an evening on the town. Decadence
drips throughout the menu from the sinful Warm Lobster Martini appetizer
to the Duck Trilogy. Dishes are prepared by Executive Chef Jamie West, with
fresh herbs picked daily from the resort's celebrated garden.*

Westward Look Resort Gold Room

245 E Ina Road
297-1151
Serving Dinner
$$$$

Gold Room
at Westward Look Resort

Charred Ahi Tuna with Asian Slaw on Crispy Tortilla with Wasabi Cream

INGREDIENTS

Tuna

1 pound Ahi tuna cut into
    1½" x 1½" blocks
2 teaspoons Togarashi pepper
1 tablespoon olive oil

Asian Slaw

2 cups green cabbage, julienned
1 cup red cabbage, julienned
1 cup carrots, julienned
½ cup red onion, julienned
½ cup green pepper, julienned
½ cup red pepper, julienned
¼ cup cilantro, chopped
1 tablespoon soy sauce
¼ cup rice vinegar
1 teaspoon sesame oil

Wasabi Cream

½ cup sour cream
¼ cup mayonnaise
2 tablespoons Wasabi paste
2 tablespoons sweet chile sauce
1 tablespoon soy sauce

8 corn tortillas

For Tuna Dust the tuna with Togarashi spice and sear in a very hot pan for about 15 seconds on each side. Cool and cut into slices approximately ¼" thick.

For Slaw In mixing bowl, combine all ingredients except soy sauce, rice vinegar and sesame oil. In separate bowl, whisk together the soy sauce, rice vinegar and sesame oil. Toss the dressing with the vegetables just before serving.

For Wasabi In a mixing bowl, combine all ingredients. Add a little water to thin if needed.

To serve Cut tortillas into triangles then deep-fry to a golden brown. Place approximately 1 tablespoon of Asian slaw on each wonton crisp. Put 1 slice of tuna on the slaw and garnish with Wasabi cream.

Chef-owner Sam Fox started his restaurant empire with this innovative,
New American cuisine eatery. Here, oven-roasted meat loaf vies for your
attention just as vigorously as crispy duck breast or an aged New York strip
steak prepared by Chef Corey Holland. The wine and spirits menu is just
as awe-inspiring and pair nicely with Wildflower's self-indulgent desserts.

Wildflower, New American Cuisine

7037 N Oracle Road
219-4230
Serving Lunch and Dinner
$$$

WILDFLOWER
NEW AMERICAN CUISINE

Macaroni and Cheese

INGREDIENTS

Macaroni and Cheese

2 ounces extra virgin olive oil

1 medium onion, diced small

4 cloves garlic, thinly sliced

2 bay leaves

1 quart half and half

8 ounces cream cheese

1 pound white cheddar cheese, grated

1 pound Swiss cheese, grated

8 ounces Gruyère cheese, grated

2 tablespoons Kosher salt

1 teaspoon white pepper

3 pounds cooked pasta (bowties,
   penne, smaller types work best)

Parmagiano Reggiano cheese,
   freshly grated

Sweat the onion and garlic with the bay leaves in olive oil over low heat until tender. Remove bay leaves. Add half and half to the onion mixture and bring to a slow simmer. Gradually stir in cheeses beginning with the softest ending with the Gruyère and keep stirring until all cheeses are melted and mixture is smooth. Add salt and pepper to taste. Mix sauce with cooked pasta, garnish with freshly grated Parmagiano Reggiano cheese. Serves 12–15 people as a side dish or 6 to 8 as a main dish.

This recipe is a great time saver for working moms and anyone who wants to be able to prepare a delicious homemade meal in a very short time. The sauce may be made ahead of time and refrigerated. Reheat desired quantity and mix with pasta as needed.

Asparagus Risotto

INGREDIENTS

Asparagus Risotto

1 pound Arborio rice

6 ounces butter

2 cups white wine

4 cups vegetable stock or water

½ medium onion, diced small

1 bunch green or white asparagus,
   medium diced

1 cup Parmesan cheese, grated

In a large pot, place 2 ounces butter and lightly sauté diced onion until translucent. Add rice and stir for a few minutes, pour wine into rice and onion mixture. Reduce by half and slowly start adding stock, while constantly stirring rice until al dente. At this point add diced asparagus and continue to cook until rice texture is to your liking. When risotto is cooked, finish with the rest of the butter and Parmesan to give a creamy rich texture.

Thank you for supporting
the Primavera Foundation.

Notes